HELICOGRAPHY

Before you start to read this book, take this moment to think about making a donation to punctum books, an independent non-profit press,

@ https://punctumbooks.com/support/

If you're reading the e-book, you can click on the image below to go directly to our donations site. Any amount, no matter the size, is appreciated and will help us to keep our ship of fools afloat. Contributions from dedicated readers will also help us to keep our commons open and to cultivate new work that can't find a welcoming port elsewhere. Our adventure is not possible without your support.

Vive la Open Access.

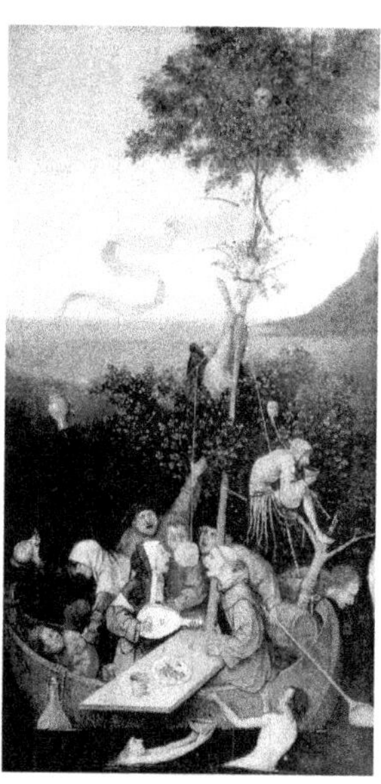

Fig. 1. Hieronymus Bosch, *Ship of Fools* (1490–1500)

First published in 2021 by dead letter office, BABEL Working Group, an imprint of punctum books, Earth, Milky Way.
https://punctumbooks.com

The BABEL Working Group is a collective and desiring-assemblage of scholar–gypsies with no leaders or followers, no top and no bottom, and only a middle. BABEL roams and stalks the ruins of the post-historical university as a multiplicity, a pack, looking for other roaming packs with which to cohabit and build temporary shelters for intellectual vagabonds. We also take in strays.

ISBN-13: 978-1-953035-64-6 (print)
ISBN-13: 978-1-953035-65-3 (ePDF)

DOI: 10.53288/0352.1.00

LCCN: 2021940246
Library of Congress Cataloging Data is available from the Library of Congress

Book Design: Vincent W.J. van Gerven Oei
Cover image: Smithson, Robert (1938–1973) © VAGA at ARS, NY. Untitled (Three Spiral Jetty Drawings). Ca. 1970. Pencil on three sheets of graph paper, 11 × 8½" (27.9 × 21.6 cm) (each). Fractional and promised gift of Tony Ganz in memory of Victor and Sally Ganz. The Museum of Modern Art, New York, NY, U.S.A. Digital Image © The Museum of Modern Art/Licensed by SCALA/Art Resource, NY.

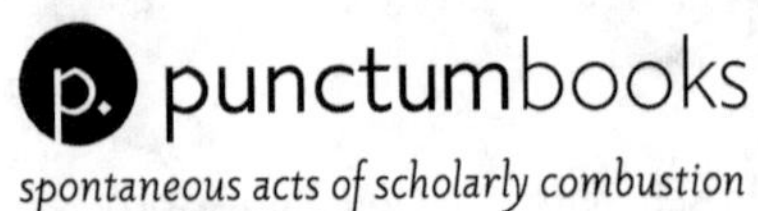

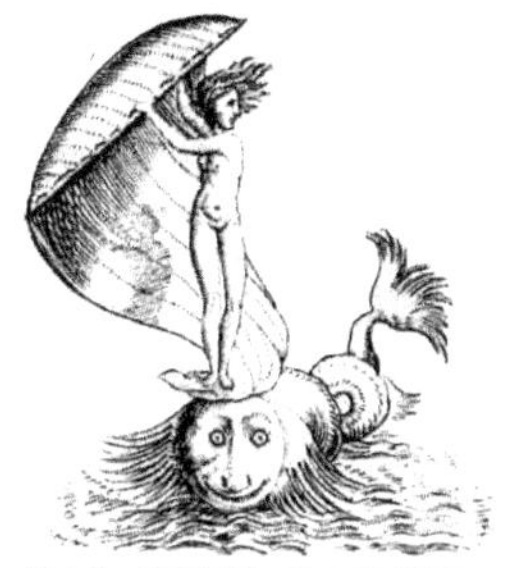

HIC SVNT MONSTRA

Craig Dworkin

HELICOGRAPHY

p.

for Stef

Contents

Helicography · 21

Postface · 135

Quotations, Allusions, and Deformations · 151

Selected Bibliography · 213

Acknowledgments

Warm gratitude to everyone at punctum books, and to Barry Weller, Aaron Beasely, and Anne Jamison for help with preparing the manuscript. Sections of *Helicography* were published thanks to Whitney Tassie at the Utah Museum of Fine Arts, Simon Morris at *Inscription: The Journal of Material Text — Theory, Practice, History*, and Stefanie Sobelle at the *Los Angeles Review of Books* — I am grateful to them all for keeping me afloat in my great salty lake of self-doubt.

Inside some stones one finds streaks which seem even more saturated than the bloody red of their background. They proclaim the circuits of planets or electrons around invisible centers or nuclei: an image of the radical law of gravity that links physical bodies together at every level of the universe. Like the curved brass rings of armillary spheres, etched with zodiacs and ecliptics and equinoctial zones, they scry jeweled bracelets for cosmographers or nuclear physicists. They reflect every phantom revolution, from the cosmic to the microscopic scale, from the vast on down, each relentlessly repeating the very same pattern. Here, in their turning, we can see the blueprint of nature itself, simultaneously hidden and revealed in a kernel of silica, announcing the blazon of the universe, revealing the persistent geometric figure that governs the entirety of creation. But in order to be moved by this pattern thus inscribed, ironically, in the heart of a stone, one needs to already know the secret it unveils or recalls; one needs to have already studied myriad scientific tomes, and learned from them the thousands of patterns which this one single figure brings together, and without which it would remain what it really is: chance curves providentially assembled by another chance and randomly colored by metallic deposits.

— Roger Caillois

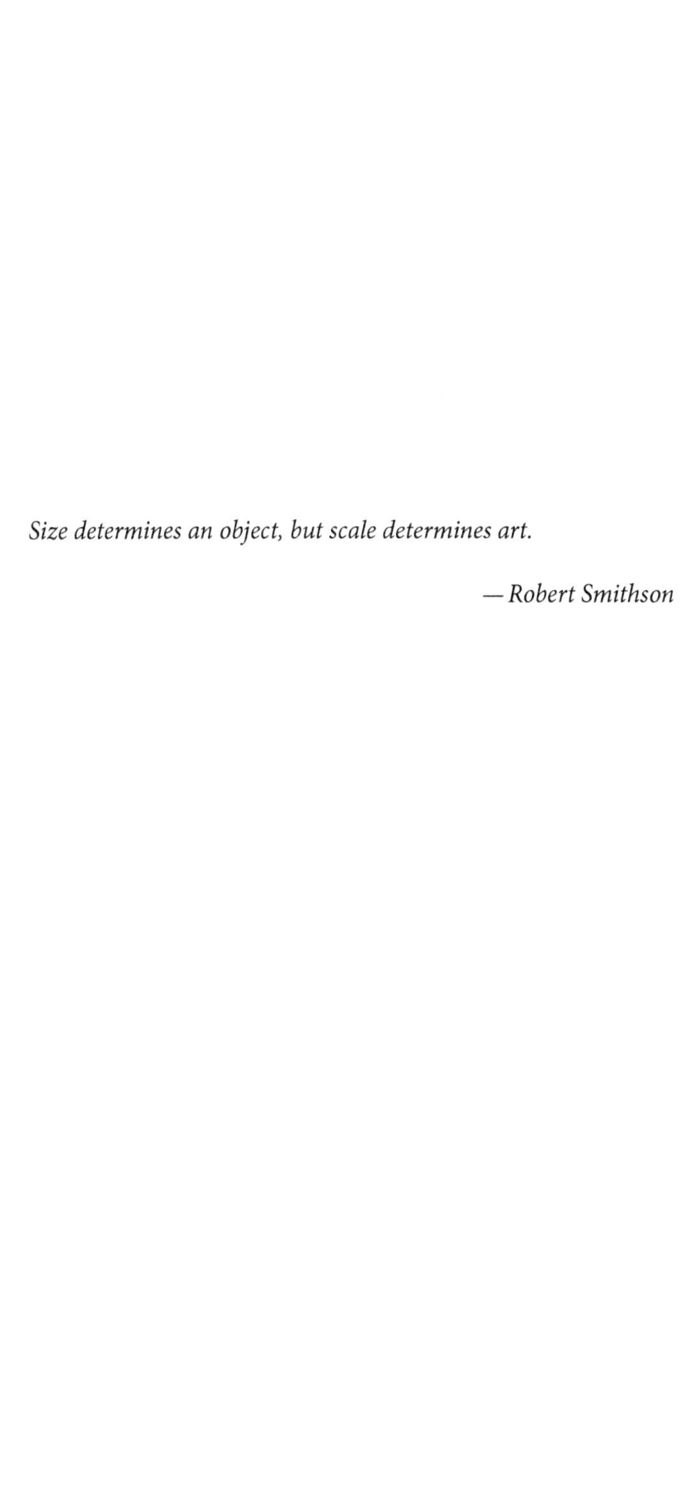

Size determines an object, but scale determines art.

—Robert Smithson

SCALE: 1 word = ½ inch

HELICOGRAPHY

Tick. Tock. Lock snap. Clock clasp clicks. Diecast cogs acquit their tasks. Gears chew with congruent, tooth-meshed, lockstep movements. Twitching in staggered, ratcheted laps of agitated fits they spin in graduated advance. A pocket tachometer of the planet's orbital engine tracks its path and predicts its lot as the taut spring's tension slackens. The eighteenth-century conception of the *Machina mundi* transmigrated from the universe to the earth itself, understood as a beautiful machine of peculiar construction: a terrene, subastral heat engine of regulated water, ice, and steam. With relief valves of pyroclasis and seismotic, tectonic shifts, the earth maintains its clockwork system, but the metaphor of the machine is a dangerous plaything, carrying with it not only regularity and precision and stamina but also fatigue and friction and deprecation: the parts warping and wearing down — bending and breaking off and melting. If the clocks that measured the motions of the natural world had been used to understand geology in turn, they were also vectors transmitting pathologies of decline: hosts to the entropic drop of torque curves, akinesic stasis, and heat death — an unavoidable fate even if earth could evade some sudden catastrophic failure, like a watch-spring brittled with repeated winds and tightened one too many times — fating it to enervation and the impotent detumescence of molecular chalastics .... with its narrative of inevitable decline, the mainspring is an elegy to time.

Since demons of lassitude lurked among the Breguet hairsprings, jeweled escapements, and golden timing screws of his chronometers, two sextants joining brass and glass with silvered scales graded every twenty minutes corroborated with doubled reflection the asynchronous rates that spread between the phases of the other instruments as the time they sought to measure passed: the Parkinson & Frodsham keeps its pace, while the Walsh slips behind in increments increasing by the day, as inevitable as the Rio Buenaventura had been to every explorer and cartographer before Bonneville, none of whom could conceive that the engine of the Great Basin — gridded with rigid lines of latitude and longitude even before it had been explored — could maintain its regulated state without an outlet to the sea, not realizing that the tributary feeds and seasonal evaporations of its lake might construct a clepsydra all their own.

But Captain Howard Stansbury, who knew better, watched the distant Wasatch pass as he piloted, serpentine, his ship counterclockwise around the lake, at ease in his prime, his personal timepiece stashed to a satchel, the company's chronometers safely placed in their soft-cushioned, velvet-lined case, prepared for the purpose, and always strapped, on the trail, with care in the middle seat of an easy ambulance or spring-wagon, allowed to play freely in the gimbals, with only a sufficient quantity of curled hair placed in rings upon their faces so as to restrict their oscillations within proper limits inside the box, bowing his head again to gaze at the sodium-coated rocks and gravel, their semblance a symbol of the waters' stillness, visible beneath the shallows of the lake as if calculating the craft of the movement beneath a beveled crystal, where the pressurized displacement from the passing hull of the *Salicornia* stirred the silt of the lakebed like callis sand — reddish and suspended in the water — eddying into swirls and reverse currents and the counter-curls of vortices unfurling in the surfless, torvid waters with the turbulent, nonlaminar flow regime of the dynamic fluid strata of the salt-chilled thermocline like the calculated cycles and counter-revolutions of cams and nested wheels before resettling, with a siren twist, in a rain of pluvial sediment felled beneath the tyrant's fist of gravity like the red alluvium of strife.

If he reversed course with exquisite precision, straking in a perfect backward circle, wake rushing in to meet the stern turned prow, would each grain rise and resettle exactly where it had been, he wondered, lost in thought, absentmindedly smoothing his hair, furrowing his brow, squinting his eyes … when suddenly, scotomatic, the sun opacified his view with an actinic glare taining the lake into a vertiginous mirror, until he was unable to distinguish light from water — the mirror kept changing places with the reflection and the reflection with its mirror in a structural blindness where all boundaries and distinctions lost their meanings in an ocean of slate, the present falling backward into a petrified sea until the sun has turned to glass and the surface of the water fused in the helium sheen of a thermonuclear crucible of fifteen-million degrees — but looking away for relief offered only the steady erosion of figure and ground, a frictionless glide of purely optical movement across the uninterrupted desert horizon and the sublation of sand to steam, air shimmering in heat, so that he was forced to admit that the crystal is the seat of greater disorder than its parent liquid in a scene where even *to see* becomes an intransitive verb and the future will have been forgotten as yet one more vanished theory, compressed and layered in the closed pages of shelved tomes, the strata of so many forgotten books — maps, charts, advertisements, art books, science books, money, architectural plans, math books, graphs, diagrams, newspapers, comics, booklets, and pamphlets from industrial companies, gaudy prints, passé literature, church Latin, erotica full of spelling errors, novels our grandmothers loved, fairy tales, little children's books, old operas, leaflets, papers, cards, circulars, etc. — until later, standing watch while the ship lay at anchor, as all the hands aligned with the clack of a midnight clap, abraiding him from his idle fancies with a start, Stansbury suddenly understood what he had never been able to recognize, the previous year, looking out across the marginal sea of the Atlantic off the Florida Keys, its waters churned by the spiraling arms of the terrible Tampa Bay Hurricane of 1848, the year of revolutions: the vastest sea is simply a desert basin in reverse.

He would issue his report on the torrid lake just one year after Rudolf Clausius published his first formulation of what would be codified as the Second Law of Thermodynamics, an equivalence value of mechanical heat diffused through the working bodies of fluids, which he christened *entropy,* from the Greek ἐντροπή ["turning in," like the coils of a spiral], a transformational content in opposition to the "work content [*Werkinhalt*]" that he took to be the etymology of *Energie,* with the transformation of the state following the disgregation of molecules, as they spread in fugitive dispersion, content to drift, preferring not to organize, unavailable for concentrated work, or what Ludwig Boltzmann, himself the grandson of a clockmaker and son of an accountant, would see a quarter-century later as the anarchic disorder into which the Austro-Hungarian Empire was also descending around him from his Styrian outpost in Graz, where the Uhrturm had struck the hour without fail for one hundred and sixty years, despite having exchanged its minute and hour hands, the regulation of the number of its strokes effected by means of a snail, and with warning signs everywhere of its noonday: Franz Joseph's little brother dead in Cerro de las Campanas; the Commune in Paris; Bakunin challenging Marx in the Hague and then the veritable schism of the First International and the regrouping at St. Imier; народники in Russia; insurrection throughout Benevento; the Spanish translator of Proudhon, of all people, elected President of Spain, where *Federaciónes* were forming; circulation of an *Arbeiter Zeitung*; gatherings of *torcedores* in Cuba, cigarette workers in Cairo, and printers in Alexandria; clubs in the barrios of Buenos Aires; the Mexicans, again, in *Congresos Generales de Obreros*; the assassination attempts on Wilhelm .... but what kind of puritanical imagination would see the perfect rest of thermodynamic inertia as threatening decline or lamentable degradation rather than a divine release from the dizzying spin of the steam-driven knitting machines turning out work without respite and without thanks, a universal refutation of the right to work as the mill wheels assemble to construct miraculous time machines, reversing the hands of clocks in a backwards blur, generating a month's vacation every seven-and-a-half minutes while the slackening winding down of every other horologe, beginning with laches of murcid and socord rhathymia, acceding to the slowing seconds' continuing attenuation, despite the wrath of lurid sermons against the so-called sin of acedia and its uncertain melancholias, announces the decay of the carcass of time, subverting the infinite accumulation of equivalent intervals, opening the way to fleeting federations of irreversible moments, until a stopped clock becomes the symbol of the ultimate triumph of playful simultaneity and the promise of a true uchronia, a paradise of exhaustion where one might dwell among the ruins of the hours, freed from the tyranny of time itself and the colonization of every tenth of a second by Capital, which took over from the parish bells and canonical hours of Religion with a zealous relish no ecclesiastic had ever managed to rouse, introducing minute-hands to clocks with the rise of Mercantilism in the seventeenth century and then second-hands with the rise of Industry in the eighteenth century, with further subdivisions to follow, down to the once invisible and inaccessible hundredths of a second snared to settle the idle wagers of robber barons who would ride toward the shores of Great Salt Lake bearing golden spikes and ties of laurel, or the constant vigilance of a scientific management that would marionette every movement of the limbs and digits of the bodies of wage-earners by steel company clerks working for mills on the outskirts of northern Philadelphia neighborhoods ....

Among the laborers who laid the final ties on the Central Pacific side of the transcontinental railroad, settled in cinder and destined to be spiked with ceremonial gold, one — nystagmic, genteel — still, though old, nostalgically recalled a phrase from his earlier trade: 鋼腸 [metal entrails], or, to be specific: "steel intestine," the term for a watch-spring, which, were it scaled to the extension of Robert Smithson's *Spiral Jetty,* would stand as a 1.625-meter-high wall, half a foot thick, extending from the bridal of the shore to an arbor around which the final turn of its coquillonage curves, to reach 1,466.75 meters, weighing over three-million kilograms — five hundred times the weight of the material moved by Bob Phillips to construct the *Jetty* — so that the force required to wind the massive spring, applied by some monumental bench key, would reach a torque equivalent to the tension needed, as calculated by the principle of levers, for the neck of the Diplodocus that freely roamed the western edge of the Morrison Formation in the late Jurassic, bending to drink among miniature forests of tree-ferns, horsetails, displotted cycadics, conifers, and ginkgos, growing over what are now the shores of Great Salt Lake, to balance the weight of its head, a force nearly enough to break *ligamentum nuchae* were the neck muscles not bearing some of the load, equivalent to the pressure exerted on the road by a Cold War-era Soviet tracked artillery trailer, or the maximum thrust of the engine of the F-111A developed to penetrate such mobile defenses, one of which collided with a Montana Power Company turboprop near Kingston, Utah, in 1974, killing the pilot, months after Smithson himself died in a plane crash, morbidly surveying the site for an earthwork to rival the *Jetty,* or the main engine of the Orbiter shuttle that would have been built in the training range across the lake from his sculpture that same year but was scuttled by NASA's decision to use jettisoned solid-fuel boosters, the survival of which required a water landing in something deeper than the shallow pool of Great Salt Lake's scant cushion, the force of each being greater than the impact of a train car traversing the Lucin cutoff, and if that torque had been applied to wind the chain to power the train of the scaled watch the spring would store the potential energy of 509,595.6 joules, the energy needed to raise one kilogram of ice on the surface of Triton, the coldest of Neptune's moons, revolving in its retrograde orbit, disrupting its hydrostatic equilibrium, from 35 Kelvin to its melting point, equivalent to one million kilograms of trinitrotoluene (TNT), or the kilowatt hours in the bolt from an average lightning strike, or one-and-three-quarters tons of coal equivalent, the amount moved per minute up to the height of a revolving screen pitched steeply enough, at about twenty degrees, to cause the coal to slide (requiring about .017 horsepower and not including the power needed to overcome the friction between the coal and the screen or to turn the pinion shaft and drive the conveyoring belt, at a cost of about twenty-five pounds of coal per hour, which amounts to .00012255 of the total coal shuttled down the conveyor in that time), or about a ton of petroleum product, or 197.25 gallons of gasoline, sufficient for a Jeep to drive over class D county roads for 3,550 miles, or 113 round-trips between *Spiral Jetty* and the Golden Spike National Historical monument, derived from 17,750 tons of prehistoric biomass — archaeans and the ancestors of planktonic organisms, algae and protozoa — despite the appeal of imagining some sore-necked diplodocus liquefied to gasoline, as the Sinclair mascot in Corrine, the nearest station for the Wrangler to refuel, would have it, and an energy sufficient to power Stansbury's watch for 2,446,058,880 minutes: as long ago as the construction of the first Egyptian pyramid ever built, for the burial of Pharaoh Djoser, in Saqqara, or the Assyrian temple in Bismya, near Babylon, or the Neolithic village of Huerta Montero outside of Cabeza de San Marcos in what is now Spain, built at the time of the first observation of Essouan (formerly Syane), the frontier between Egypt and Nubia, to be directly under the arc of the Tropic, at the moment of the founding of the greatest university of the ancient world, in Heliopolis, near Matariah during the twilight of Elb-Havel, Bernburg, and Globular Amphora cultures, replaced by Corded Ware and Single Grave cultures contemporaneous with the origin of Dravidian languages, according to the latest phylogenetic studies, just as two Koryaks split from a common subclade ancestor in the Haplogroup C-M48 of the Y-chromosome DNA, while Thylacine, pouched, disappeared from the Australian mainland, coinciding with the introduction of the Dingo, a span measured by the half-life of isotopic ^{18}O, or the life of Alerka, rival to Prince Yudrishi, as the sacred authority of the Sama-Veda vouches, which would make his age 115 x 30 or 155 Seds, while the demigods have 300, or 10 Seds, the gods 2250 or 75 Seds, and the Cynic cycle 2100 or 70 Seds, thus firmly establishing a mystic factor of 140, or the sum of the average life lost in Denton County, Texas, due to premature death, or by Latinos in Boston, or the average period of the modulation of the 1,800-year oceanic-tidal cycles, a span that would stretch back to the end of the arid Holocene climate and the return of humidity, the time, some reckon, using population-doubling algorithms, from the biblical Flood, when rhyolitic tephra erupted around Lake Taupo, in what is now New Zealand, during the New England Elm collapse and the last iceberg-triggered Florida Pine burst, when the seed of what would someday be the world's oldest, continually standing tree, a bristlecone pine in the snow-coated fault-block White Mountains, was first implanted in sandy soil surveying the Great Basin below.

The snake strikes. The clock strikes. The miners strike.

A rough granular crumble adds a facture to the calcified hoodoos raised in stocks and stones above the flats and fractures the light through miniature forests of prismatic foliage, arithmetically accumulating, to execute with its kaleidoscope of bone-snapping powers a fraction beyond the reach of any language, an excecation pixelating carcasses and carapaces coated in skeletal abstractions of crystal-covered elemental forms; arthritically articulated and mortised in place, the grotesqueries — like specimens in a medical museum of lapidary pathology — all posed in torsion, frozen in a ballet of *rigor mortis* above the crust, stage a morbid scene of azoic topiary gloating with the equivalent of cranial grins, as so many gods of wood and stone, abandoned by the estuary drain.

The encrustation of all abandoned objects on the pocked and dented plain scries the post-anthropocenic with a bleak portending of its torpent epoch.

Thin residues of nucleates condense on any surface left exposed. Laminal strata of sodium chloride columnate, supporting the entablement of the etiolated sky. The sun abacinates all daring gazers. Come dusk, cautious scavengers in serfdom to the shore will scurry in the gloom, carrying away *stipites* and *pabulum*, restocking their stores. Two isolated pyramidal pillars, of naked freestone rock, the resort of sea birds and the breeding place of encroaching eagles, rear their vast fantastic summits to a considerable height, substituting air, merging with the sky, disarranging the perspective at that formidable altitude with the retort of their holohedral forms, and strike the eye of a stranger, in approaching them, as the sunken piled spires of some old submerged cathedral. Their attitude accessorizes the hillside down which boulders, over eons, cumulate.

The styles forecast the passing hours.

Twenty thousand years ago, an ice age chronicled the quartzite in grooved striations, its frozen cryospheric script inscribing lines as if composing some epic literary work planned and commenced with pensive, coplanar, petroglyphic iterations. With the power and solace of lithic patience, the glacier pulled up boulders, stripping the fields with an austere scour and polish, breaking and loosening the surface of the ground, redepositing rocks as the ice sheet made its gradual retreat across the pedosphere in a slow-motion catastrophe of forced migration: fallen, transported erratics in a scatter-plot pattern of random distribution discernible only from a fully graticulated atlas, with an inframince *intermundium*, coextensive with the unscaled territory it claims to map, projected at a one-to-one ratio.

The same process, in miniature acceleration, took place across the baked edge of the dry lakebed by the now extirpated species of *Oreohelix strigosa* once endemic to the region, in simple streaks of slow erosion as the snail's ambulatory passage wimbles the pebbles, detaches the topsoil, and rakes the sand with its forward thrust, fanning the jumble of various grains—like tailings of waste rock mined from a quarry—into a lapidescent wake. The lithic tillage araches. The silt forsakes its crust. Tracks are taken for symbols.

To move from the *Jetty* to the receding waters of Great Salt Lake today would take the patient creature thirteen-and-three-quarters hours (the glacier would have required a full decade to outpace the race of the water's decline). The speed of snails remains independent of their dimensions, and so even if the precipitation of calcium carbonate forming its shell accreted to the size of the *Jetty* it would neither hasten nor prolong the journey's span. But enlarged to equal the measure of that mineral ossature, it would be culpable of other distortions. The ocular bulbs at the top of its twin pronged eye-stalks, for instance, in causal interaction with the pantomime of light and shadow in play across the lakebed, would be ninety-six times the size of the pyroclastics ejected by volcanoes above the slopes of the promontory hills: cooled into alkalic basalt boulders, skidloaded, and dumped by Phillips into the salt and sand suspension of the lake's shallows where the crude seeps, unseen, oozing to the surface from Pliocene deposits beneath Rozel Point.

The snake charms; the clock chimes; the hammers chirm.

The shadow of a gull wing briefly shades the scene; tentacles flinch in phototaxis.

The snail creeps with an incremental, pendular cruising: extruding and clenching; surging and quailing; exposing to risk and quickly recoiling, proffering a body that's just as soon rescinded; heeling, thus, with a determined lean into the wind, it approaches the shore in even measures. The single foot, mucus-lathered, slides over a discordant intrusion of igneous rock with roughly oval cross-sections and steep sides, somewhat smaller than a batholith, each pebble paving the pelopate path. The creature propels itself with the bobbing nod and lazy indefatigable rhythm of the counter-weighted head of an oil-well pump.

It passes over clover pastures, ungrazed and choked with helianthus. In stately stride, without haste, in his sumptuous ruffe, dermis writhled with corrugations and then taut with stent extension at his greatest height, he shall be stocked in full many a straight, though few get to witness the entire relentless commute, or sit through the incessant rehearsals of graded inertia, or fathom the *tempus fugit* refusal posed by the foot's ungartered, guarded pace — in limpid hose at once both lubricative and adherescent — of its spatial traversal.

Rocking in sync with the wash of distant waters the gastropod undulates in tropotactic locomotion. It rows through the sand like an oarsman in a skiff.

Thin wisps of fricative wind thrust with rapier gusts, as if to say: "and if a horned diuell should burst forth, I would passe on him with a mortall stocke."

The shank of a hawke tenses, anticipating launch.

Lymph absorbs the lipids of the chyle.

The snail's ommatophores swing like inverted pendula, impelled by the weights of their ocular orbs, grandfatherclocking. Each counters the arc of the other's pivot with a cautious, mirroring parry. Their crossed épées sway with the *graciosa* feints and clever barba cuts of open-and-shut dramas endlessly replayed.

Remontoires register regular intervals.

Gulls rehearse their commonplace phrases.

Two cranes, with their long shankes staulking full untowardly, mimic the pivot and sway.

Spotless and sombre egrets saunter with similar step.

Curious waders move forward, pecking away at artesian secretions from receding breakers with artisanal, scimitar beaks.

Interested, at first, and then taking an interest, investigating, before giving full credence to some new stimulus, invaginable *ocular* peduncles retract with a reflex reaction.

A thick liquor of red-wine brine stains the runs of the inlet's eddies. Dispersed seeds leave an emulsion of cellulose substrates exposed in the kallitypic sun.

Emulating their leader, the entire portion of a pelican fleet, floating, gauring, gazing, jesting, laughing, mocking, pointing, sporting, talking, torturing, align along rails towards the vanishing point of their elegant, migratory formation.

Stems inserted in graft upon trunks attach at an angle like quill feathers cut to a nib for writing with ink. The sap seal weeps and draws from the lesion.

A bit of straw, a "mote," in sunlight winks as it floats in the draught.

Laid up, provisioned, the pier piles rise straight as the stale of a ladder, the petiole of a leaf, the pedicel of a flower, fruit, or inflorescence, the stip of an ovary, or the like.

Flocks pratter and rap as the grasshoppers happer the dried pattern of tiles cast in cracks when exposed evaporites, exsiccating, contract.

Vertiginous, Stansbury, parched from heat and deep dehydration, sees the shore fissures, apophenic, morph into a nightmarish series: a roller for a map, a perch for a bird, the hasp of an alms box, trough, or wherever the cloth is placed to be beaten by the faller, or mallet, or brace, as with the beater in a scutching mill, or a swarm of bees, or a wool-card's wooden head, or the handle of a fowling piece or capital distinct from revenue, principal from interest, the stipulated from the foil, endowment and dowry and the wealth of nations in the whole of every whit entirely.

Above the bedraggled, talcomicacious crust, all distance disappearing in the waning light, the metasomal mechanical motion slows like the cementing flow of volcanic tuff across the pedregal field: the entropic fate of all matter in its suspended cosmic flight.

The basic mollusk, in translation (a perfect calque of *metaphora*) across the great basin, toward the fine limn of its chalked meander finish line, slowly approaching the brim of the shore's scored curve with a calculus of closing approximation, continues to pick up pebbles with its viscous tread and redistribute them, with gradual absumption, across a surface recalcitrant, calcinated, callous, indurated, weathered through long exposure, and frosted in a sodium snow.

Beneath the breme, keening winds the tack of its track sheens the matte of the plat with a subtle sateen.

The cautious and vulnerable result of *Stylommatophora* shelled, coiled, torted, and pulmonate, in a long race of vertuous Ancestors, descending from *mollusca* antient and venerable, over millennia, to this single pedigreed specimen, cousin to the common *Helix pomatia,* in slow roam endures beneath threatening sun and the even more ominous shadows of circling birds in avian scavenge.

At long last attaining the shingle's strand, where the edge wave, at home in its narrow margin relicks the shoal in sinusoidal laps, the snail falters — petrified, dangerously sunned, stunned stiff and benumbed and stunted in abrupt halt stoken, standing, withering with the sequent lysis, contracting in the osmotic shrivel equivalent of a sudden desiccation, its final sensation, the last thing it feels: the pervasive sting of the tender, cauled membrane from the saturated salt of the brack, piquant waters of the vast desert lake.

Lashed in the sand, as if an anchor hauled to by a tackle and tightened, locked fast in the pan, the calcium-carbonate epiphragm seals with the adhesive operculum unique to the clade.

Eyes lock, hands hold, hammers chime.

Still, in its turning, the sun—tangent at the peak—rakes the saddle of La Sal pass, down the west side now, touching the ridge so the tussocks stand out, in tufted hummocks, like wide nests for clutches of the last Titanosaur, through the light sandy soil pouring toward Paradox and on to Bedrock. Water rails and vagrant crakes with instinctual volition trace the Colorado back toward the long-baked hard-packed pan of the alkali flat, like some orating Cratylus prattling, from their beaks, paiking with an iron screech the brattling that excoriates to make nerves raw from restless gnawed insomnia in the final push to Promontory. Spiked ties trek below the tracks below the roods distracting from the open stretch of road with wires webbed from pike to pike. The substrates of communication meter out the space they have contracted.

Below their path, the world from worry, melt, abrasion, rot, and shock decays. What's left will rust. Everything not outright plundered has already, in advance, now been betrayed. The earth rasps on; chronology razes; around everything not openly surrendered, the mills of fate revolve with invisible, measured leisure, imperceptible, indifferent, but with the burrs of its inexorable crush set exceedingly fine. The ratchets granulate and pulver. Any lubricant eventually renders. Ravines incite a ravening imagination that cannot conceive of any acquisition that is not simultaneously an annihilation, extermination, or dispossession.

With a migratory pace straddling the strake of the plates that fold the valley down and thrust the Wasatch up and over the travelers return through airy routes that mime the waterways which burst to vein the quaternary plots of seismic scarp displacements. Subsurface traces of the Willard thrust in the downthrown western block of the fault-cradled creek in its continuous crop uncomfortably overlain by Tintic Quartzite floored by low-angle faults of basal folds over glassy basalt sweep past, intercalated, exhibiting extreme brecciation and flocced by scattered clasts once blasted out as shot rock by the Southern Pacific for the shoring of its causeway buttress, shaling above a fragile crust of vitric tuff.

Damped by fleshy pink entrails of eviscerated fiberglass, spilling from a field shack, and past chimeric, ambiguous, amphibious tracked contraptions, the sound resounds. In the silent absence of a specimen, seventeenth-century accounts imagined finger cymbals or the tiny tinkle of small bells, figuring a *tintinnabuli* of timbre not of form. Some fancied the tone of running water to be the goal, attracting thirsty birds, others that the locust buzz was lure to hungry birds, a miracle of gulls in search of swarms of shieldbacks but finding an Edenic fate among the viridated shade of early summer hills. A measure of molten chronology solidified as albuminoid accretions from each slough, the caudal instrument keeps time. Its interlocking keratin is stacked, compact, but with sufficient play to swivet like a castanet, a cascavel or cricket, as strident as intense cicada thrum — a dense, spasmodic, dance to generate a humming buzz at once both harsh and frantic: the sound of corn in granary or in a pile outside, the ripping of calico, the roar of falling water, the sawing sound of tools on wood or of a whirled stick. The vehemence, which starts full force sustains with an electric, live-wire severity. The quartered quavers mirr and dadder.

Crows, at a loss, veer and disappear.

Diapsids acupate. They rink, approaching to an apsis and await. The hour elapses. The salt air wafts. A delicate bifid tongue flickers for attention with its winks.

The pioneers believed that snakes, unblinking, with a slight sideways waver to their lofted heads, could hypnotize their prey. But they failed to consider that the snake itself might be beguiled by the prey at which it gazed — entranced, transfixed — venom seeping like sap through its fangs as a sort of fatal Pavlovian saliva. But the tocsin of its tail — tremulously premontory, aposemic — blurs, by its harmonics, as it monishes, the line from *avis* to *avis,* "warning" to "bird," a visagra for a whisper, a visage for a whist, the rese before arrest. Trepidation cues from crepitation. A narrow outward curl on the edge of every lobe doubles back, flattening, to form a sort of selvage, and serving as a clapper to the bell of the loosely clutched and interlocking keratoid cloaks. With a cadence of vibrations somewhere between the rate of alternating current and the heartbeat of a newborn baby, pitched in microtones between an A# and a C#, the speed increasing with the heat, the rattle frequencies achieve a hiss from overlapping stochastics as the rapidity of hollow, dry collisions agitates the tapered lobes, dislodging any fundamental root.

Bellwort, they believed, was an alexiteric to the bane.

Unexpected, ekplectic, then in abeyance — the sound, it is hard to remember, hypostasizes kindness. Altruism made audible, the alarm does not denote the fearsome pride of some maleficent draconic threat, but is rather a symptom of the reptile's own perturbed panic: the musical expression of the amygdala. And then, rough music of its rapid clatter gone unheeded, it sibilates with sudden aspiration: the hiss of a reedless, wind-instrument finale in imitation of the furious percussive overture drone.

The snake itself is deaf to the sound of its own rattle — as well as to the treble of its histing gasp.

(Incredible, considering the tremble, to think that *aspen,* collapsing, ouroboric, the flutter of its leaves like a silent rattle and their shape like the head of a snake, teethed at its extremities, is etymologically unrelated to *asp*.)

In a single season on the shores of Great Salt Lake, the rare and occasional appear: oldsquaw, common loons, a great egret, an Eurasian wigeon, Bonaparte's gulls, great horned owls, a merlin, and a whimbrel. In the burning surge of perpetual heat, discerning birds, diasporic, descry herpetic patterns in the faceted aspect over which they pass. Optic nerves process outlines on the pavement of the pan; they search for safe landing with an optative scan. Above the ground strewn with cindered fragments of obsidian the salinated air sprinkles its minerals like sea spray while from underneath asphaltic oil seeps through turbid, sigmoid sands — its crusted layers irreversibly compounded — mixing to mark herpetographic passage. Streaked and puddled with oil, the grains absorb the ambient noise; the only sounds come from a few gulls and the oldsquaw's mate, which drifted down the polluted channel from the lake. Among the xeric scrub and matchweed broom, limber pine and prostrate juniper, between the saline stands remaining from the Bonneville regression and late glacial pluvials, the squamate winds its ophidian paths, flanks channeling between the raddled stalks that strew the storm-caked matted drift, sticks twisted to hurdles hedging like a wrathe rake combing the warp threads of the desert text to make a maze of hazel-lath wattles wove between posts, clattering in wind like the thrash of bones, in lateral traversal of its palatial demesne, ingluvious, scraping over an asperity of lithic scatters and flake banks from some terminal Pleistocene accumulation of once stemmed and hafted lanceolate shapes mimicking the viper's own javelin head and sourced from as far as the exploited flows of Topaz Mountain — then carried to the ancient lacustrine meander following the terminal drainages of anastomized and complex braided narrows entrained to dermal furrows furthering the channels across which some Leander will someday swim to meet its hero.

Aspherical errants and pyroclast basalt make a sport of symmetry.

Brine flies blight the sky in billows. Wavering air absorbs the passing humid vapor. Hymenoptera paralyze the dipteran. Orb spiders weave for paper wasps. Predator and prey swap places. Phalaropes forage for brine shrimp; the pipers reck and jab. Wide-eyed, asphyxiating, the mouse in the mouth of the snake makes a final, exasperated, blasphemous heave before collapsing—its last sensation, deep in the dorsal muscles: an addled ache. The jaws unclasp. The mandibles begin to ratchet. A jackrabbit pauses at the outward quiet, then launches—the hare's hinds scatter, patterning the ground's mosaic of luteous dust, white quartz, and blood-red jasper.

Behind the curtain of the foothills, somewhere in the Dugway Proving Grounds, a swivel-mounted Gatling rakes the dunes.

This naked terrain, these negligent spaces, consecrate what fear it is, lewd as is, that humans still feel from the fold of the sinuous, when what the absolute owes is surrender. The lacustrine desert: its weird and commanding beauty; its subdued and godless coloring; the baffling intricacy of its fearless designs. From the shore, the clean, unwavering sweep of rounded spiral whelms the creeping undulations of serpentine forms that writhe in artistic profusion of lacertine convolution. Far from the inhabited capitals of the old northwest, Stansbury heard the ominous whirr of a villanous-looking adder as it struck, another was thought to have killed a mule, another killed by his men among the rocks, but he saw only one other snake while he was upon the lake itself. He imagined that it would soon return to dwell among the prairie dogs and owls, peaceful sharers of their subterranean retreats.

In Stansbury's time, a rattlesnake was thought to strike two-thirds its length. Coiled at the scale of *Spiral Jetty,* the range of that elongated snake would span the Mississippian-period

Chokia mound, the world's largest earthwork, which in the time before Columbus was the third largest structure of any kind in the Western Hemisphere, a continuance equal to the perimeter of the outer curtain wall of the Frankish fort on the spur of Mount Kallidrom, guarding Thermopylae, and taken by the Turks in 1410, a compass comparable to the promenade of the secluded olitory at Monticello designed by Thomas Jefferson in his retirement from Presidency, which protracted to the reach of the cable that had tethered Henri Giffard's balloon, the first railway station between Paris and the Moon, at the Universal Exhibition in 1867, a loft as high as the stretch of the Duluth, South Shore and Atlantic Railroad Company dock built at the L'Anse ore port on Lake Superior in 1873, or the 1888 municipal pier in Naples, or the brick B&O warehouse built in Camden Yards between 1898 and 1905, then the largest building on the East Coast, or the Gatun locks on the Panama Canal, which at the time counted as the largest machines ever built, equal to the unit length of the fixed-block system of Inter-Borough Rapid Transit track between signals, or the standard extent of a single gold claim in Eureka Creek, Alaska the same year the subway opened, or *Stewart J. Cort*, the first thousand-foot ship, launched as Smithson left the States for a sand-mine at the terminal moraine of a long-vanished Ice-Age glacier that cut the rugged spine of low-lying hills that angles toward the North Atlantic, marked by vertebrae of lateral-stone-capped megaliths, to ply the Great Lakes for Bethlehem Steel to carry 58,000 tons of taconite pellets to Indiana plants on the dunelands of Burns Harbor.

Eighteenth-century biologists tended to favor a shorter strike, and would have expected such a serpent to have hit a mark as far as the tallest of the great sand dunes at the foot the northern Sangre de Cristo Range of the Colorado Rocky Mountains, or the lateral span of the Pont de Neuilly, built in 1774 by Jean-Rodolphe Perronet, painted in 1890 by Albert-Charles Lebour (now Musée de l'Île-de-France), and demolished in 1956, at a point at which the Seine has the same width as the Harlem river, which was the length of the *Pequod* or the height of the Trylon spike indexing The World of Tomorrow in Flushing Meadows or the twin towers at One Columbus Circle — tours of the monuments of corporate World Wide Web media — the extruded extent of the biannual linear yield of a garden spider's thread.

The average reeling yield of a silkworm cocoon, in comparison, would measure out the distance calculated by more conservative recent estimates of the relative accurate strike range of a rattlesnake, which would pitch the point of safety just past the vaulting soared by the fairy-spire ribs of certain Gothic cathedrals, which rise to the height of the snow accumulated in a dozen years in the Cascade Range, which equals the annual retreat of the Quelccaya Ice Cap in the Peruvian Andes during the late twentieth century, matching the annual advance of the Portage Glacier in Alaska, the distance leached each year by the Ogallala aquifer southeastward through sandy gravel beds and by the Étang de Vacarès southeastwards over low sandy ridges in Provence, the monthly progress through a standard drift of soft hematite in the Marquette Range, or the peatland dredged in a day by Minnesota homesteaders, which is the fixed distance spun in a single minute by a steam engine geared for rolling sugar cane, which equals the ground covered by an aircraft initiating a constant descent-angle approach, or the velocity required to cure tough pieces of bacon by an automatic injection machine, which was the space travelled per second by the bullet at impact on Governor Connally's wrist, after impact with his rib, after impact on his back, after impact on John F. Kennedy's upper back, or in other words: the speed of sound in water.

Earlier naturalists, basing their belief in part on exaggerations from the Osage, who told tall tales to gullible intruders, would have steered clear of any *Jetty* snake by a bowsprit measure of the biggest oil tanker ever built, or kept a clearance the length of one of the biggest dams in the world, the famous Croton River dam, now equal to that of the Perrine Bridge, 486 feet above the water of the Snake River — the highest cantilever structure for its length in the world and a destination for building-, antenna-, span-, and earth-jumpers from around the globe.

We may be best served by approaching scale not as an ontological structure which "exists," but as an epistemological one — a way of knowing or apprehending, as with the measurement of anger, or lust, or fear at the sound in warning along the creek bed, where the snakespiral springs of the mattress's brass quoits and pendent viper radii, loose and tremulous, shed flecks of rust and leach selectively to a slow corrosion of rococo variations on the seech of surf as if in imitation of the rush of waves upon the shore, beating up the skiffs and cliffs, and skimmington of the charivari of a dubious wedding day, sounds rising and falling by fixed intervals, ringed keys to the compositional locks that regulate the tidal levels, their octaves divided by laddered staff lines scoring the page of the stand, including an indication for an antique hautbois, overcoming the summit, ascending the heaven hidden and shaded by enveloping mist or haze, as if scorched by brume, as pelicans in maniples, squadrons, or battalions sail over the Point, the constellation Libra overhead, shining with the interstellar product of light intensity and time required to give an acceptable variation in density to the scene in a film of oxides stripped from metals of the mesh of a net to gather gill-bearing aquatic craniates, with the intent to defraud, to guess the amount of timber standing, or stacked in logs where what is shed, as in a hut of heaped peat or the custom-house of a seaport town, is massed in middens partially burying a dish, a cup, a goblet, a husk, pods, chips of stone from shale, the ratio accordingly of the width of an organ pipe to its length in the distance mapped by a Marquois rule applied to the minute structures forming the covering of the wings of butterflies in dance among the loose substance from a mine or quarry including errant ore leaving only a rocky stratum denuded of soil as from an earth-slide during an excavation and bits of argillaceous fissile rock in fragile and uneven laminae above bitumen with its pattern-converging crypsis of compact, granulated, lamellated, fibrous hydrous magnesium silicate flaking like a dermal disease and precipitating out for a considerable time to something without value, like the empty pans of a balance — an attribute, like blindness, of Justice herself as they fall, with the dense drops of mercury tears, from her unseeing eyes.

The snake rattles; the clock strikes; the miners strike.

Even the systems of physics are historicizable: the recovery of scrap copper requires a smaller consumption of raw materials than the mining of ore only under certain, specific, given circumstances. The very delineation of molecular matter is bent and distorted in order to define order so as to distinguish between a piece of electrolytic copper — the kind used for electrical cables, more essential to modern life than any other metal — and the same copper molecules diffused so as to be of no use to us: emolumento of the automatic shuffling of the sieves of time, with its framed screens in continuous shake — gradually spread to the four winds. Copper, the Mercury of power and information, the translation of the symbolic, takes wing.

Chemistry is the alchemy of Alchemy.

Metal is more verb than noun.

All the machines in the Kennecott operation at the Bingham Canyon mine are cogs in a larger entropy engine, moving from raw ore to refined metals, grinding away in a rotating mill of whetstone rotation and fine-sand polish to hone the lanceolate barb of the arrow of time.

But the tip never reaches its target; the half-lives, like some Zeno's paradox, simply shorten. Even the history of media in its most material form points not so much to disuse as to ever more costly recovery. The history of copper mining, with all of its environmental horrors, extends to the salvaging of wires stripped from the mountains of inoperative machines that accumulate as communication infrastructure abandons cupreous metals for glass and plastics engineered as optical fibres smugly gleaming at their refusal to lose information in the way metallic wires radiated meaning and absorbed noise as if semantically uninsulated. Obsolescence leads to accumulation; information proliferates material; a mountain of copper mined outside of Salt Lake City slowly diminishes while a mountain of copper rises outside of Foshan. Humans, monoxenous, parasite the planet as they signal and sing.

The deep time of modern communication stretches back past the prehistoric compression of sea life into carbon fuel to the geologic time of mineral formation, but it also arcs forward to the future fossilization of everything we abandon back to the geologic. The future, fueled by the mined, returns underground (as in the resistance imagined in Chris Marker's *La jetée,* the last ohms of history in tunneled bunkers — fugitive, desperate, masterful). The geophysics of media powers a clock that measures past the human.

A few years after engraving a great spiral on the torso of his infamous King Ubu, Alfred Jarry — writing as Dr. Faustroll — published "Notes to Aid in the Practical Construction of a Time Machine," a popular-mechanics assembly guide so detailed it was taken by readers, hypnotized by its convoluted precision, to be a genuine instruction manual. Several wrote to complain that although they had followed his directions to the letter, their time machine was not functioning.

At the heart of Jarry's temporal engine is another spiral [γῦρος]: a gyroscopic device that works something like a film projector to charge the media of the luminous ether, animating individual photographic stills to produce a motion picture, like the one premiered by the frères Lumière, in which duration is the transformation of a succession into a reversion, or its inversion, in Marker's motion-filmed stills in *La jetée.* The projector, spooling and unspooling spirals of film, is the time machine that transforms trucks into dinosaurs; the archaeozoic medium, suspending precious metals in strata of deceased herd mammals, transports the filmmaker into the earliest-known geological eras. The editor pulls lengths of film out of the movieola with the grace of a Neanderthal pulling intestines from a slaughtered mammoth.

A sudden chime rattles the mind.

With the formication from some mescaline dream, excavators scoop the earth in recurrent circling laps, like the burin of Claude Mellan, excising spiraling filings up and away from the copper-plate — lifting in splinter-thin miniature skyrockets, with festive curling flurries — in a confetti of streamer shavings, replicating in three dimensions the curved path of the graver with their helical DNA of negative space as he forges the icon of the sudarium, a miraculous pressure-print veronica, unfolding with an inspired mockery of the guileless beneath the air, the art of the artless, in a monumental subaerated defile, perhaps as when a revision slips out of control and what began as some minor adjustment, to account for a wavering error of the hand or a quick slipping skid of the style, requires a counterbalancing correction elsewhere, and then a return to keep the new whole in check, and then just a touch on the other side, which, too much, needs a bit more to compensate elsewhere ... until the first mistake is the only part of the picture remaining that looks at all right and the work tips over into a grinding cancellation of frustrated revenge against imperfection; or perhaps Mellan was mesmerized with the same loss of focus that the engraver's prints were said to produce in his viewers, as their magnified concentration on the technical virtuosity of delineation caused them to lose sight of the very image that made that line marvelous in the first place — peering too close, losing the forest for a tree as the force of the wavering line breaks free into abstract swells and narrowings, like a phonograph groove's visual, silent sonics, as the picture blurs; or perhaps he was adrift in a reverie of religious contemplation and devotional rapture, a lapse from ecstasis, gazing into the eyes he had drawn of his Savior who, once summoned, drew the chalcographer in in turn with that infinitely deep lamb look, at once unflinchingly and scathingly judgmental and completely forgiving: twin pools of lacquer black behind the graphite metallic grey of supersaturated, intensely concentrated arsenic seeping from the stare until unwatched and unattended the automatic hand had rounded, repeatedly, to gouge and blind, disfiguring, in a passion of dervish circles adding a new torment to the thorns and flails, vinegar and prod; or perhaps he had simply discovered the wonders, or infernal horrors, of a pure abstraction and seen from the first chiseling scratch the inevitable telos of a logic that once unmoored from figuration was destined to end in its own self-consuming destruction, as when the rationality of a grid on a map sinks into what it is supposed to define — a *reductio* of annihilation that constructs the very black hole whose gravity is so great that no inscription can escape it, even once it has made the desperate struggle to break free from the heavy ballast of the dead weight of the real world — but in the first cut, in the terrible violence of the sheer unsignifying mark itself, Mellan had drawn the zero of form, the ring of the horizon, the circle of things from which he could thenceforth never break free.

The Mexican border funnels southward, retreating from Utah like a film, in reverse, of the shoreline of its inland seas, animating the littoral as political with retreating demarcation.

A moth slams onto the mirror pane of a glazed window, as if dizzy from circling the candle in a frantic attraction to the trigger of its reflexive rebound.

Cartography colonizes the microscopic, as terrestrial mapping extends to the masses that amalgamate and fuse to rise above the waters of the oceans, and then closer, to those lapidary constituents of the earth itself, delving beneath the crust, and then beneath the hardened skin of lithic fragments, beneath the carapaces of creatures with billions-years half-lives, which thrive as nothing but skeleton, and where the skeletal vibrates from core to surface, compressing the mercatorial geometry of the gridded globe into the condensed charting of the axes and faces of the angular vectors and intersections of planes that coincide to describe crystals. The mind x-rays the stones that once insulated the very minerals — buried beneath the southern Utah sands — that enticed the imagination of a penetrating vision in the first place with their radioactive vibrations. But crystallography, in turn, leads to mapmaking, and the survey grids of USGS cartography relace the landmass with a crystalline structure.

The raddle moon rises; the hour falls; the picks mine.

A pock so vast on the face of the earth that it is visible clear from space with the naked eye, the manmade canyon mine spans four kilometers from side to side, and even from the brim the fleet of million-pound hydraulic haul trucks — grinding on twelve-foot tires, which will wear smooth within the year — oversized but proportional with the prehistoric logic that led to gravigrade sloths and mammoths, seem like specks against the sets of concentric paths as they crawl with the relentless pace of collective insectoid patience and resolute purpose, recording their past havoc like the teeth of inset clock gears. The drones convey the stones in widening gyres unraveling to describe a slope of over thirty-five degrees; the cone opens wide its landslide hands of graveled ochre sand to hang its upturned gambrels on the slabs of desert sky. During days it drains to an etiolated cirrus; the troposphere, curing in the earth's reflectance, dries; October sun retracts its ultraviolescence; the aspens, deciduating, cope.

Counting towards the doomsday of their own collapse, the excavators open to view, with a mockery of displacement, the conical space of an immense, reverse hourglass: removing rather than accumulating countless grains of sand with the straining dray of shovel-loads in long-stint rounds of scoop and haul and dump. They accelerate the aeolian processes that slowly erode all landforms in the Intermountain West with an abrasive, sifting, slow displacement. Exhaust fumes, cumatic, further shimmer desert air in waves of gaseous carbon, nitrogen, trace carbides, and solid matter mixed with sulfates. Peering, arachnean, with eight four-thousand-lumen halogen headlights clustered on their fronts, the haul trucks crawl continuously throughout each night's half-day shift. The sump waits with patience under the gaze of those crazed pneumatic clocks.

The terraced turnings of the tracks stack to graduate a conic section cut into the Oquirrhs' eastern slope. The concentrating rings shrink, contracting as they sink. Seen from the valley, the century's slow sculpting wills a strange, strict geometric face: a countermountain introversion, overburdening the range. Between the mornes and linking saddles, it corkscrews through the forks and chutes, and goes from magnetite through molybdenite to bornite chalcopyrite down to lesser pyrites that seam to bottom in lead zinc. The proper core may never yet be reached. For over a hundred years the porphyry deposits have supplied a quarter of the world's copper, along with collateral fortunes in recuperated lead-silver, placer-gold, platinum, and palladium.

The Guggenheim fortune came from this copper, along with other long-shot bets on low-grade deposits from enormous mines like Chuquicamata and El Teniente, in Chile, and vast slabs of Alaskan ore. The low yields were thought to be uneconomical, but Daniel Guggenheim realized that the value was only a product of scale and a quasi-infinity of time — continuing to mine when any other engineer would have concluded that the site had been depleted. Where others dug for years, the Guggenheims persevered for over a century, despite declining grades. The problem was never quality, but volume. Their mines expand as the metals dwindle. The business model is the projection of an economic equation which spirals like the strip mines that sustain it, narrowing to a point as their circles expand.

The excavation tracks model the museum built for them by Frank Lloyd Wright, which might have been cast from lost-wax scaffolds of the strip pit that funded it. Indeed, the millions allocated were not enough to cover the copper-colored stone exterior Wright had proposed.

But the connection to the earth was even more direct. Instead of quarried earth, erected as a monument to the mined, the building was a work of mold rather than chisel: its ready-mixed concrete façade not even fabricated by architectural contractors but by civil engineers. The Euclid Corporation expanded on the geometry of the ramps and interchanges and curving cloverleaves of the post-war American interstate highways and the dazzlingly engineered elevated roadway—known to Port Authority as The Helix—that spun Smithson out of the Lincoln Tunnel into New Jersey on his trips home, or to the quarries of Great Notch and Upper Montclair, bringing the poetics of the building back to the roadways of the excavator trucks that tirelessly circled to cover even George Cohen's winning bid, which still came in a million dollars over budget. A Temple of Spirit to Non-Objective art, the building is an architectural index of the Bingham Canyon mine, a realist rendering; it has more in common with the genre of landscape painting than the geometric abstractions it would house. As the museum director understood when it was unveiled, the building was birthed from the earth rather than any lofty ideal of the spiritual element in art; he threatened, if anyone criticized the architecture, to have it screwed back into the ground.

There, even the disseminated copper-ore body lies in a vertical cylinder of shattered and altered monzonite.

As the new building opened its doors, the Guggenheim holdings, consolidated as the Kennecott Corporation, began aggressively pressuring private homeowners in the Bingham Canyon to sell their land for pennies on the dollar; a smelter purchase integrated the operation, transforming the ore on site into saleable anodes; an eighteen-thousand-foot haulage tunnel was completed, cutting the cost of circuitous upgrade drayage. In tandem with the nationwide steelworkers' strike, at the time the longest work stoppage in U.S. history, the local Utah unions idled mill and mine and smelter that August. They were strike-bound for almost six months. The year that had begun with record-high production ended in a record low.

Every communication over twisted copper wires carries the faint hum of its history: eviction, massacre, expropriation, exploitation, disenfranchisement, alienation. Their derivation is a product of the last electric age, following the discovery, by Faraday, of electromagnetic induction; the telegraph wires that webbed the west extruded from the Bingham Canyon lodes, and continued to spool out into twisted telephonic cables, carrying pulsed codes and voices racing faster than the trains beneath them, panting as they smoked and hoping, stoic, to keep up.

Telluric currents pulsed beneath the nineteenth-century deserts, generators of technologies and expeditions.

Ostensibly serving its human exploiters, the mineral phylum and its byproducts in fact finally codified the tragic epic it had collectively composed; the molecules recorded themselves on the biological substrates of the bodies that sought it: the warping calligraphy of overextended skeletomuscular systems and the distended chancellor hands of deformations from malnutrition exacerbated by excessive caloric expenditure; metallic sediments accumulating in tissues and weighing down the keratin with its spectral signature; zinc and lead leading to sinking; dust settling deep in lungs, writing down its laments in lampblack lines; neurotoxins rearranging chemical alphabets, misspelling protein sequences, garbling the codons; salts rendering mucous membranes coriaceous as a parchment page; kidneys hijacked to broadcast coded slogans and victory signals; toxins contaminating cells with their graffiti scrawls; metallic dust lacerating the tender sponge of pulmonary tissue; carcinomas embossing the bones with braille patterns; tears laced with sulfur dioxide streaking the cheeks in long *sōsho* characters. The acids and gasses in their caustic vapors scorch the dermis and scar internal passageways with the disregard of settlers carving initials in bark or scratching dates on boulders to mark the demise of yet another wilderness border. The chronicles of the earth are written on bodies with residues and dissipated remnants, etching themselves into the scraped and wasted palimpsests of organic pages.

Then again, there are those who say the copper was desperate for the telegraphs and telephones that needed it, the gossip and commercial negotiations that yearned for it, the rapid chatter of human language that set it free from deep subterranean dungeons, liberated to vibrate at long last and not caring that it never understood the messages it carried.

The museum, a mirrored displacement of the mine that spirals like the *Jetty,* owns both Smithson's *Yucatan Mirror Displacement* and *Hotel Palenque,* a slide lecture delivered at the University of Utah, where he was a Visiting Professor of Architecture in 1972. The walls of the Mexican hotel, its empty swimming pool, the blocks piled for construction in a vernacular Minimalism of primary structures were all, like the Guggenheim, of concrete. On his return to the States from his travels in the Yucatan, Smithson undertook a *Concrete Pour* in Chicago.

The clock strikes; the snake coils; the miners picket.

The patient, gentle, archaeological brushes of the wind reveal the shape of a buried dotaku, rattling rather than resonating in its ritual of apotropaic sound, warding off locusts in hopes of good harvest, and planted alongside crops, cultivating a cupreous patina of Greek green like a lichen of acids and scales.

The cyclone stones of *puquios* open over aquifers. They channel katabatic winds to raise clean water. Evaporative vacuums draw down breezes; their currents stream to speed the springs. The Andean rain shadow harbors trenches which had gone unmentioned by the Spanish for four full centuries.

Horizontal wells reach water when it migrates from the zone of infiltration.

Following the unicursal ingression circling the Dantean layers, in a narrative arc of gradations through infernal degrees, toward the noisome sulfur fumes of future smelting, the creatures rehearse a glaciated epic of retreat—constructing not an open-air natural history museum of fossils and ecological data but a fossilized museum of the aborted, surrendered, prematurely clipped, and pruned possibilities of a topiary tree of life—its myriad contortions tried on in the costumed *tableaux vivants* that froze for the photographic flash of a million lost apocalypses. Eons here have been compressed to individual still frames in an animate film: a glaciated temporality in which the wrecks of death are but a change of forms. Some whorled shells have rolled out into the hall of minerals. The excavators churn in an arid cyclone of acrid extraction. They slowly smooth the pages out on which the twisted script of fossilization is written: a cursive of spiral shells, inscribed as an epitaph into the headstone of the mountain so that the entire terrestrial sphere is a cenotaph as grand as Étienne-Louis Boullée's, in which the corpse it would contain has been displaced to form the marble of its own tomb.

A capsized temple bell, unclappered, sounds its meditative call to contemplate Śūnyatā. It focuses the silence of the Great Basin that contains it. And the void that contains the basin, in turn. And the emptiness that cradles the void. And the hollow beyond. And the vacuum that follows. And the inscience of it all.

As prospectors sought the seams at which to open up the Bingham Canyon mine, a giant temple bell was being forged near Ise, but would not smelt—and then the molten copper would not pour, and then the bellows could not raise the heat, and only with the kindling of a copy of the twelfth-century 血盆経 [*Ketsubonkyō*] thrown into the foundry furnace did the temperature rise to over a thousand degrees, so that the metal would melt and mold into a flawless form, with a magnificent sound.

The *Blood Bowl Sutra*, long pressed into the service of misogynistic propaganda, warns, at its heart, against the pollution of the earth from human overpopulation. The ferrous blood that seeps into the soil returns as copper and iron, rusting the waters that are drunk. In the blood pool, it was prophesied, countless insect-like creatures with metal snouts come to pierce the skin and worm in spiral tunnels. Interior and exterior, human skin and terrestrial crust, fold in on one another under the liquid logic of rock in fluidity: excavation and flay; accumiated tattoo and puteal bore; twin wounds that meld in a weeping, sympathetic hydrology.

The earth thickens with blood and waste; the body turns to lead. An abstract geology distributes itself across chthonic and biological substrates.

The reversals and inversions recur in an endless dynamic of eruption and enclosure. A point on a map expands to the size of the land mass; a land mass contracts into a point. But cartographic accuracy and legibility are inversely related. Detail defies comprehension; comprehension obscures precision. Even Phillips's carefully staked lead lines, measured to exactly 1500 feet, expands as one focuses in — tracing the waver of the wound twine, and then up and down the crimped facture of its woven strands, moving out along the frays and inward through the splices, a corrugated route of rise and saddle through ravines and steeps of ruffled undulations from furrowed cinch to fiber summits, detouring around impassive lint and bouldering dust, then inward and expanding further to the bouncing buffeting of molecules in branching, locked assemblages, channeling toward rollercoaster waves of pull and push from forces acting in the maze of spaces between particles that charge and orbit in disorienting traces patterning locations more probable than ever known — until the distances accumulate to more than any estimate initially assumed.

माया [*maya*]: from the verb "to measure," or perhaps "to disappear," "to be utterly lost"; what is constantly transforming, like the paths of atoms, or the unending stripping of the mountain down, and therefore spiritually unreal; the epithet of Lakshmi, goddess of abundance; hence buried wealth or hidden treasure, like gems and precious metals deep beneath the earth; knowledge turned into illusion; concept made manifest; an idea in physical form; art itself.

Suppose that a magician or a magician's apprentice were to perform illusions for the crowds in a subway station. Clear-sighted sceptics would inspect it, poke around and prod, think it through, investigating, look behind the curtain, and carefully consider it from every angle — and it would appear to them to be void, hollow, and coreless. For what core could be found in *māyāya*?

The precious stones that hide themselves, that bury themselves — the flowers that stare brazenly and exhibit themselves ... alas. And the sorceress who kindles her coals in an earthen hollow? She will never tell us her secrets, nor of everything we cannot guess.

Petals pour in autumn storms. Helianthus rattle on their pedicles.

The sonic connection between the metals of the drills and diggers and the ore they percuss, fettling the walls of the quarry with a rhythmic, orchestrated scour, raises its colotomic chorus in a syncopated gamelan that serenades the slopes. The glare of verdigris tinging the tracks shades the shadows as the stone rings, echoing.

The rapacious greed of humans may be boundless, but the scope of their impatient clawing toward the mantle of the planet can be calculated as a series of conical sections. The irrationality of π, despite its constancy, in measuring the circumference of each level of the mine as a ratio of its diameter, provokes a deep Pythagorean terror when the infinite appears to spiral in the form of a periodic phenomenon that cannot finally be controlled. The secret knowledge requires conspiracies of silence, a refusal to tell us, to unearth the instability of the ground on which logic rises, and the seepage pool at the center of the stripped pit waits to drown any rebel acousmatic who would dare divulge the irrationality of numbers, or confess to the incommensurability of the side and diagonal of any square revealing the limits of the language of mathematics to express the world it has built: the unspeakable, the unnamable, ἄλογον — a Pythagorean surd.

The mine sinks, by steps, like an inverted ziggurat to some forgotten empire in theocratic thrall to the worship of annihilation. Stepped like a Mayan pyramid, climbed downward from the inside, one rung per day, to reach the level at which sacrificial blood leaches up through porous floors, filtered by the limestone sponge of lithic alveoli interceding in divinely breathed, elemental, alchemical exchange, the mine is a temple to negative space. The razing by its tracked pneumatic priests enshrines a geometry of absence. It measures the earth with its own displacement. Already deposited in the archives of geology, available for operations initially inconceivable, was the model of what would later be an alphabet. Each stratum is read by the augur: pages of gramaryes encrypting the vestige of arcane, occult knowledge are pried from the press of their soiled boards. Inscribing spaces with their palpable absence, the architecture commemorates not by the durability of its sturdy permanence — a monument carved to stand for ages with its solid mass of stone — but rather by its cancellation of space: an emptiness key to Maya architecture, where meaning enters, anchored by surrounding mass, extolling void with new prestige.

The one who enters stories, stratifying, in stepped laminae on which the sun leapt with bounding stamina, through every year's day's trajectory — and promises, theoretically, to do the same again. The wealth amasses. The acids stagnate. The ore is smelted. Tailings accrue.

Augers bore with acute perforations, pricking the flayed skin of lesioning sores.

Machines pummel the earth with an incoherent guttural language of fricative growls, voiced gratings, glottal stops and hard plosives in a chatter of rubble and gravel with rattling phatics — erratic, cacophonous, continuous — constructing a tunnel of Babel in the negative space of spiraling ramparts, colonnade shafts, and lateral gutters. Persisting, with hybris, they aspire to dig deep enough to match any tower ever imagined — a pyramid balanced on its inverted apex, a katechon of negation and innovation invoked in a language of mute impediment — to someday finally reach the abode of their gods of jumbled confusion and scatter.

The strip mine is an amphitheater for viewing its own tragedy. Like a crumbling ruin at Delphi, the terraced *cavea* stand vacant; the seats of the benches are emptied of spectators and prowled by protagonists masking as actors.

A quarter of the Oquirrh is quarried for ore. The synchronous pack shadows and flanks. Mechanical predators circle their prey. Their pathways round in draconian coils. The minerals flake from the shanks of the drills. The fangs of the shovel mouths chew at the loosened. The seepage pool dankens, brackens, and beckons reflection.

Scales snike; springs coil; beeles bite.

Since it opened, the sunken spiral of the Bingham Canyon mine has supplied almost twenty million tons of copper from porphyry ore. Even if it were brought down from atop its mountainside and reduced to *Jetty* size, it would still have produced 653,168,000 dollars' worth of modern pennies over its lifespan:

the currency value of all the many gold and silver nuggets mined from Colombian canyons between the mid-16th and late-19th centuries (in 1889 dollars), or the gain in foreign trade for Great Britain from 1895 to 1900 (an almost 80% increase), which was the annual world exportation of cotton manufactures in another five years (primarily of clothes, but some 15% each finished goods and yarns), which a decade later equaled the value of Indian rubber and gutta-percha exports to all the countries of the Americas, or the average export surplus of the United States in the first three months of 1945 (by 1988 it would be the surplus just to Turkey), which was the total capital outlays for resource development in 1947 (including expenditures by the Rural Electrification Administration for projects in the desert southwest), ushering in the prosperity that would fund the investment equaled by the aggregate net gains of persons conducting retail and wholesale trade establishments in the State of California in 1961, which was Mexico's total monetary reserves in September, a decade later, or the foreign-exchange reserves held by Pakistan in September, 1985, the same year that it was the cost of producing 416.5 million dollars of value (assuming the prospect of a 30% opportunity-cost of capital, according to intricate emulation models) in the copper-rich Andes, where the insurgent Shining Path massacred as Yma Sumac warbled with an Incan, thereminic tremolo over octaves to magenta mountains.

Apache-basket weaves of willow fill and empty endlessly on form's own accord. Piñon pitch seals the switches. Grains, contained, ferment. Yucca stains the vibrant spiral stillness with an earthen red.

In a day, skilled modern miners could excavate from the *Jetty*-sized mine ninety-two-and-one-quarter tons of raw material, the same rate at which fertilizer was produced in the easterly sewage district in Cleveland by the end of the Second World War, solidifying shit to liquid gold with a mock alchemical transformation, or (to keep to the geologic rather than the biological) the amount of sundry unclassified minerals and ores exported from New South Wales in 1892, as Therese Malten sang Kundry in Bayreuth, or the same weight of toys, games, and sporting equipment assumed drayed by rail to the United States in 1988 according to federal carload waybills, including Nintendo Systems and Pictionary, which over the pace of the same time frame matched the output, per person, of Indian coal miners at midcentury, all of which would have been required to heat the Glace Bay Public Building, in Nova Scotia, in 1922.

By the time the open pit of the *Jetty* had been stripped to catch up with the Kennecott, it would notionally be 47.52 feet deep, equal to the grade per mile of the Mississippi below Davenport for some distance, the maximum grade ascending south on the San Joaquin & Tulare line, the shortest radius used on a maximum grade of an 18-degree curve on the Ohio Southern Railroad in 1887, the distance moved, as recorded by slow-motion video, between the time it becomes necessary to stop and the time the vehicle begins to slow down before entering a skid, a ratio of contrasting discontinuous durations of collapse, the length of the shaft between inductors on the starboard side of the Steamship *Harvard C.H. Peabody*, or the seventy-two-hundredths chains between point F and line KJ in the contested sector of the real property as marked on the Plaintiff's Exhibit in the action to recover lots in the Town of Hector on the east shore of the Seneca in 1958, the distance south from the center of the track, on the west side of the wagon road, at the corner of the fence, two miles south of Cambridge and five miles west of Glasgow, where the road crosses the Chicago and Alton tracks just as it enters bluffs going west, where a copper bolt in the runic scribed B.M. stone sets a benchmark, which is the maximum depth of the Pleistocene marine deposit known as the Yerba Buena Mud, or of the flood gauged at the Pont de Fleurs about twenty miles above Roanne on 18 October, 1846, which reached the average height of the five-span bridge above the bed of the right fork of Peter Creek by Kentucky State Highway 632 at Phelps, or the center-arch height above pool stage of the Wylie Bridge of the Union Railroad at the Channel span of the Monongahela, just at the point of the more recent cresting of Lake Houston from flooding in the San Jacinto River on 26 June, 1968, as Iain Baxter proposes an "eroding fountain" to Smithson, who is traveling to the Franklin Mineral Dump in New Jersey with Michael Heizer, who had just begun making his *Nine Nevada Depressions,* the same month Smithson publishes a proposal for a "Hall of Destruction" in The Museum of Leftover Ideologies, to be built just beyond the sickly lagoon known as The Slough of Decayed Language, in which to house some bones from Hannibal's elephants.

The lake level, sinking inexorably, falls further and away, tantalizing, as the moisture sinks below the surface of the sands and the saline concentrates further toward what will one day be only a single, lachrymal drop. Perhaps these sunken lagoons simply remind us of the drowned world of our uterine childhood, but they generate a thalassic thirst and yearning for the surf. The astringency of the loss triggers the spray of the mouth's own buccal tides, a compensatory wash to allow the swallow of the salt of our internalized tears. We consume our sadness in the desert. It wets without slaking. The runnels slough their sinuous liquid skins. We wallow in the loss. The eutrophic retreat triggers a psychological regression. Phylogeny deconstructs ontogeny. The stratigraphic laws of superposition lead to a petrification of the subconscious itself. Not only is the prior always somewhere below, but it must already have solidified. A paleontology of consciousness looks back on the ossified paths of its neural past. With Nicolas Steno's proposal that time is directional — a catastrophic cycle of deposition, submersion, and cancellation, in which the past is downward, and hidden by the layer of the present awaiting its petrification by the future in turn — the principles of psychology find their repressed origins in seventeenth-century geology.

Minerals and crystals, encrustations and veins, all once flowed in a slowly stiffening liquidity; the heart of the earth beats with the hematic pulse of copper, which remains in our own blood to transport oxygen, in a prophecy of our future calcification, carrying the essence of the air along ferrous paths like a molten mountain through lava tubes beneath a flow-field skin.

Steno began his geological studies with a dissertation on the teeth of prehistoric sharks: *glossopeterae* or tongue-stones embedded in rock to reveal a lapidifying virtue diffused through the whole body of the geocosm, revealing that much of the earth itself is organic matter, a once living lithic.

The teeth of extinct selachimorphs, with their distinct foliated architecture and nested rows, opened by uplift to the purview of natural scientists, not only connected the quick to the saxum, but the present to the past. The dentition that survived the cartilaginous melt of tissue into silt strews like rose petals pressed in curving petrose paths. The scutes of stegosaurus fall like leaves from amputated spinal branches. The terrestrial clenches in trismus. Roots impinge the spongy loam. Opaque cases for the display of enameled relics, limestone domes house halide phylacteries for serious halidums. The stony extension of the sunken earth's trenches turns out to be an enormous jaw for holding the teeth of extinct terrors. Teeth gleam in lapidary mandibles. Set in limestone gingiva they masticate the past.

Steno also discovered the parotid gland, source of serous salivation.

The snake watches; the gears teethe; the mind recoils.

In its first year of operation, the *Jetty* mine, with its curving design like a basket of harvested earth, a chthonic cornucopia of minerality, would abound with 134.92 pounds of Copper, utterly free from Beryllium or Topaz, exactly the amount of potash, valued at $5.40, in the fertilizer for wheat-bran rations compared with silage rations in the Hatch Farm dairy-herd experiments conducted in the winter of 1904, or the amount of fertilizer, with substandard levels of phosphorus, nitrogen, and potassium used in the mid-1980s per hectare in Ecuador, or the same rate-yield of opium in Uttar Pradesh in 2006, the amount of cocaine seized from a private vehicle by the Canadian Border Patrol near Blaine, Washington, in March, 2003, the estimated per-capita consumption of meat in the late 1920s, the projected per-capita consumption of beef and veal in the United States in 1980, equal to the amount of Sotra brand Cold Smoked Salmon Fillets, vacuum packed, pre-sliced, and ready to eat, contaminated with *Listeria monocytogenes* and distributed to market in 1994, the lightweight cutoff between feather and welter for boxers (where Dingaan Thobela, Rose of Soweto, hovered, wavering the needle on the official scales), of Billy Sherring as he left the cold of Canada for a Grecian summer to run the marathon course in the 1906 Olympics, of gold champion Ben Hogan, the upper weight of the uncertain measure of a talent, the net weight of an Ohio Brass Company Porcelain Wall or Roof Insulator (part No. 10655), and the strength per square millimeter of Cammell & Co. compound armor plates, which was the average weight of an Amherst college student in 1890.

At the same time, ninety troy ounces of gold would be garnered as the supplemental bonus to this aeneous quest, an aurichalcum from the orichalcum: the amount in a United States military Atlantic-theater escape-and-evasion kit, to be bartered in the event a pilot were shot down behind enemy lines, including a one-pound and two half-pound Sovereigns (of South African mintage), a twenty and a ten Francs coin, and three rings; equivalent to 266 tolas; the average in a ton of bonanza ore from Henry Sunde's Mexican San Jose de Agujas mine; the dosage loaded per ton with a strong acid cationic exchanger, according to resin analysis by fire assay; the weight of the Honourable Roddy, professing to be the largest gold nugget in New Zealand, discovered in 1907 at Ross; the result saved from the dross during the demolition of the Wharf mill in South Dakota, produced by reef mining at the Sultana claim, south of the old Jimna township, in the 1940s along the sunshine coast, or at the head of Peter Creek a decade earlier; the average yield culled from Superior-Slave and Yilgarn-Pilbara cratons in Archaen terranes per square kilometer; the high yield reading per ton claimed by Thomas Moray, in Salt Lake City, for his exploratory "electrotype-therapeutic" X-ray curing of ores, aging them prematurely with breeding reactors, through valves of triboluminescent zinc, powered by an inexhaustible energy source: a cold form of electricity which sympathetically stimulated the oscillations of interstellar radiation.

That gold is bought at the cost of sulfuric acid, a byproduct of the smelting process, which in the year of *Jetty* mining operations would accumulate 204.75 kilograms of H_2SO_4, which might instead have been used to prove that acid concentration is not a limit for the leaching process, rising without losses, or added at 60° Baumé to a sulphite liquor and mixed intimately before being briquetted and fired to 518° Fahrenheit whereupon the binder decomposes leaving a pure, solid-carbon skeleton, or drained as waste mess from the cap at 38° Baumé from the new Kessler apparatus modified at the turn of the 20th century, or used to delint a ton of cotton seeds in a twenty-minute treatment, or sprayed over a hectare for the optimum promotion of *Phaseolus* groomed for starch formation and photosynthesis, or required following a fuming acid wash to purify twenty tons of Russian lubricating oil, or tubbed as a bath in which the finest pitchblende-filtering residue can be left to stand for several weeks at normal temperature (or better, elevated temperature) until the color becomes uniformly grey, or applied as a regeneration level for breeder nuclear plants with cation units for each depleted cubic meter.

And still, despite the caustic acid cost, the wealth without a doubt compounds; in just one year the *Jetty* mine would yield all the silver projected to be sealed in concentrates from Bulldog Mountain, north of Creede, remembering that *jetty* and *projected* share the same root, as does *projector*: the film and its apparatus thus linked in the history of Roman projectiles unerringly finding their targets in the crystal haloids of substrate and subject. Every year the silver from a *Jetty* mine would be sufficient to manufacture four hundred prints of Marker's *La jetée*, or three hundred and fifty prints of Smithson's *Spiral Jetty* film, or thirty-five copies of Alfred Hitchcock's *Vertigo*. These renewals of dupes and prints are requisite, since the life of any film is finite: every screening opens the strip to oxidation — accelerating its aging and the attendant brittling, shrinking, and twisting of the celluloid into unreadable helical dead-sea scrolls — along with the weakening of its splices, the smears from aerosolized sprays of oil and thick streaks of motor-coating grease from the projector, through which it scratches as it runs against dust and microscopic debris, dirties, and from the humming vibration of its rhythmic spin and guillotine gate chips at its extremities' edge and tears its sprocket holes until it flaps, lacks the tension needed to keep beneath the narrow clearance of the guides and rollers, rides roughly through its looping course, and speeds itself toward the realization that every screening illuminates the image of its death. Disintegration is the cost of vision, and payable at the rate of the thousandth of a gram of silver in each frame. Any given print survives only a few hundred runs through the ravenous chewing of the apparatus, and so any single cinematic image survives for only one and one-third seconds before it disappears, unviewable as motion picture ever more. As Marker argues in his jetty film, one cannot escape from time, and narrative cannot escape its substrate, but time itself has a substrate, and time is measured in telluric units.

If that film, on 16mm stock, were unspooled to the length of the *Jetty*, it would just perfectly accommodate Andy Warhol's *Blow Job*, Jack Smith's *Flaming Creatures*, Kenneth Anger's *Inauguration of the Pleasure Dome* (first version), Werner Schroeter's *Neurasia*, Robert Nelson's *The Great Blondino*, Numasawa Isezo's *Ishi No Uta* [*Cries Coral Reef*], Margaret Tait's *Caora Mor*, Mauricio Kagel's *Duo*, Stan Brakhage's *Song 23 (23rd Psalm Branch, Part 2)*, Paul Sharits's *S:TREAM:S:S:ECTION:S:ECTION:S:S:ECTIONED*, Dave Lee's *To a World Not Listening*, Les Blank and Skip Gerson's *Spend It All*, Rajendra Gour's collected short films, Su Friedrich's *Damned If You Don't*, Bashar Shbib's *Or'd'ur*, Maja Weiss's *Juwes in Slovenia,* Gordon Matta-Clark's *Open House,* Jodie Mack's *Dusty Stacks of Mom,* Ernie Gehr's *Side/Walk/Shuttle,* Jem Cohen's *Chain X Three,* Peter Greenaway's *A Walk Through H: The Reincarnation of an Ornithologist,* Yamamoto Hyoe's *A Glance Apart,* Yasuhiro Omori's *Wedding Ceremony in Bali,* Pavel Korec's *To T Trat'* [*This Is the Track*], or any number of industrial, documentary, and educational films, including the Richfield Oil Corporation's *California and Its Natural Resources,* which shows the transformation of deserts into productive fields by irrigation, coasts into petroleum-producing regions, and mountain slopes into mineral mining and milling centers.

The snake springs; the clock winds; the miners wound.

The wine, archiving the history of its terroir, concentrates calcareous soil to bloom.

Is there measure on earth? There is

None.

Measure is only a convention, an intersubjective agreement which is the condition of merit (a social recognizability of material available for value). Verse conspires to set the metrics by which its own deviations can be judged. The terms condemn the statute's words and assure that every failure in fact compacts success. Contrary to the expectations of meter, poetry is actually the excess which breaks the limit of its metrics and escapes valuation. In that fugitive moment, a democratizing parity establishes relations — concatenations of equivalence — that render scale meaningless. The abolition of scale opens a space of abstraction: fluid, amorphous, form without determination.

The shape of a drape of cloth in an air current initiates a rhythm.

Things exist; we don't have to dream them up. We just need to grasp the relations between them. And the threads of those relations are what form poems and orchestras.

Every other science than Logic is the science of certain concrete relations. Logic, however, is the science of relation in the abstract — of absolute Relation — of relation considered solely in itself. An axiom in any particular science other than logic is, thus, merely a proposition announcing certain concrete relations which seem to be too obvious for dispute.

Despite their light, the stars cannot illuminate the bodies that deflect their paths. They pale before the gravitational stygian. The textile fringe of waning forces frays, forgetting both its origin and destiny. Railing in an incoherent fulmination against the curtain that hangs between observation and inference, between what we can see and what we can measure from the curve of infrared light, one realizes that when one refuses to release scale from size, one is left with an object or language that *appears* to be certain; scale operates by uncertainty: the hazy, the vague, the indistinct, ill-defined, lazily passed-over moments of plot in favor of details that refuse to narrate but ask merely to be read.

Filming backwards as the truck moves toward the future jetty site along the ungraded dirt and gravel sideroad toward Rozel Point, Smithson was able to make visible entropic time: an ever-expanding and -receding cloud stirred from the tires in billows of obscuring dust — a plume in churning spume that will eventually settle, one assumes, in an equivalent distributed stillness, a pollinose road indistinguishable from the one first encountered, but with every particle now in a different location.

The truck deterritorializes the earth as atmosphere, along with scattered biomatter and a haze of pesticides and agricultural chemical traces, including the dispersal of the machine itself in the process of dispersing the dust of the road in swirling clouds that make momentarily opaque the particulates that always already invisibly cloak every travelled route: lead and chromates from tire wear; clouds of carbon soot mixed with hydrocarbon gasses and fine flakes of nitrates, sulfates, and other metals from the super-heated exhaust pipes; brake linings worn to friability and diffusing a microscopic glitter of copper, zinc, and lead; the exhaust of tired constituents sent to drift dreamily back to rest on the roadbed. The wheels calculate upon the abacus of an eroded slate. The air hangs heavy with its displaced geology. Ground level is always somewhere above our heads.

The scene also prefigures the murky turbid waters of the lake and all those galaxies — clouds of nebulae, including our own *via lactea* — that will inspire the spiral shape of the sculpture to come, that has already formed as a notion in the natural motions that would hypnotize the mind of the artist blinded by the western desert sun reflecting on the *lacus mortis,* intensified by the million crystal lenses of suspended chlorides.

The analogies provoke a reinforcement and prolongation of spirals that reverberate up and down space and time: a spidery ripple of arms spinning webs of manufactured time warped among pulsating galaxies; amplitudes slackening, vibrations dissipating, cepheid variables throbbing; a shadowy and fluctuating domain, now shrinking, now swelling, in accordance with the vacillating energies of the imagination; a precession of forms; the sweep of waves on a beach made with dust from spiral galaxies; the sound of the universe carved into a dot; the torsion of the organ of Giraldès, the line of sockets staring blankly from a heap of skulls; the weeping *salix*; the phidian rhythm of a frieze; the frozen tears of bouldered stones sobbing from the eye of a petrified cyclone storm.

The winter quells the pace of brine shrimp breeding. Shells turbinate like whelks. Hyalinosis vitrifies the corneas. Flaws mature to fractures.

Steno's law without leniency applies just as much to astronomy as to geognosy, and so the milky way is thus itself a kind of chronometer.

The differential rotation of the disk risks desynchronizing the rates at which the matter circulates in eddies between the intermediary rifts. The center swells with age. Small-amplitude waves propagate with a uniform angular velocity; patterns of enhanced density compress the gas and stellar dust as they pass the differential paths of luminous matter rotating slowly at the periphery compared to the faster spindle of the center.

With living matter, in contrast, spirals accrue from concentration: a mutating ladder of twining helices achieving the natural efficiency of a maximum compacture—biological density expressed in form, the form described mathematically by the Fibonacci sequence, the series's terms establishing the frequency of segments in a field: helianthus seeds; the chambers of a nautilus, the scales of a pinecone; the whorl of petals around a sepal, the torsion of a cumulative shell; the umbonal swell of biomineralization that leads to pearls; a phyllotactic pattern in the texture of the bud.

The *Jetty* seeds ideas in the clouds of rational expansion; the analogues precipitate. The clouds shower in low curtains of mist and fog, to be sure, but they also collocate: the rim of a caul; the darkening fall of sulfurous particles in the amber of urine; floccules in quartz and other mineral formations dulling their translucence with diffusing diminution; sebaceous densities in the sheen of the lactic; nacreous patterns suspended in semen; the abode of the dead.

The lake laps; the clock hands clap; the mine collapses.

Beneath the low, stern sky, gravity impinges rain in the meander line's slack canvas. Seen, by turns, as attenuating, opaque streaks and discrete hollow cavities, the droplets briefly dark-en sand but do not soak—evaporating as they land. A Morse Code of precipitation signals the secrets of early autumn in the intermountain basin. Nebulous semaphores flutter as they form. Virga quaver and measure out their rates of vaporization; emerging from the horizontal floors—combed by their own motion—the branching bands accumulate from heaps of altocumulus. Condensation coating desert dust and salts afflates, alated, before defaulting to the fate of every body. Like a miracle, debris mimes geometrical precision; calculus approaches its etymology. Cataracts threaten, and then contract. The floodgates of heaven throw open, then close, the vertical slats of their latticed windows in bands before the sun. Chimerical, the matter metamorphoses like glass from sand. The ventral surface rounds before the dorsal; a spherical contour appears; the downward reversal polishes and melts. Fugitive granules pelt the earth, demolishing distinctions between states. Weeping from the weight that they cannot escape, tears weave their own tissue and sublimate without remorse.

The pine siskin feeds on thistle, the acanthis on thorn; the thraupis signs. In the alphabet of leaves, acanthus forms with spiral serifs. Prismatic silver sulphide paramorphs after argentite; the acanthite spikes in the Cactus and Sheeprock, the Eagle and Bluebell strewn among the Tintics, the Mammoth and Sunset, the Gardner Adit and the Satisfaction Occurrence, the Snowflake.

Graupel rimes the winter crystals. In other seasons, constellations of conditions generate a hydrolithic instant as the updraft cools precipitates while windshear hones the ice to hailstone. Even on the most arid days, tourmentes of alkali dust dance across the flats in miniature whirlwinds, murling the friable earth in a weaving Ghawazi sway of sinuous hover, suave feint, and sudden shimmy.

Integrating the rates of a lacrimal calculus, observers slowly learn the punctual, acute, strategic crypsis of inscription; the pattern of the patter describes the nexus between the tempestuous motion of the storm and the form of a fossilized cyclone: atrophic; indocile; withered with a pseudomorphic mineral infolding. The facture of sharp shards and abrasive pumice gives way to rounding. Sockets eventually pock the curve at points of displacement, denting the plain. Both the fangs and the alveolar processes begin to be absorbed. Cracks reticulate the tissue of the silt, situating a honeycomb of tracks within the widening gaps between tilted boulders sinking into soil. The dentistry of erosion breaks the stand of the stones, bending the pitch of the whistle of the wind; phonetics rearticulates in turn; the velic opens and the plosives soften. The ground incorporates. The cut of the guttural canal damps the ring of the gamelan. The falcate shape concatenates its boulders like lordotic vertebrae — a burial case for aching ganglia — into a vortex forged against the gentle swelling of the shore. It braces against the relentless wash that carries away the base of its foundation. Aeolic verses record a relic of the stresses. Ebb, press, recede — the inventor of harmonies flows, heaves, and razes, before an echoing close count of nearly even inscribing; measured, archaic alcaics tide tides.

The alcarraza of the basin swells, imperceptibly, as it sweats and cools; even in nocturnal temperatures, a tyranny of aridity dominates its desert caliphate.

A falcon's flight crests the hilltop, dispersing prey.

Sulphates of copper stain the drainage with chalcanthite.

The status of the sculpture becomes a victim of cartography. Receding waters leave it stranded, no longer in the lake. The lease is lost. The stones should be returned, by law, to the slopes of the hills from which they came. The idea is marooned in an impossible legal space.

The movement of the stars triangulates the navigator on the lake: empirical; empyrean; pyramidal.

Scale begins with the passional vortex. Both *earnestly* and *rational* translate *igitur, ita, itaque, utique, ergo* [so, thus, therefore, consequently, hence, in any case, at any rate, assuredly, certainly, by all means, unfailingly, indubitably, at least].

A self-enclosed rotary of gyrating space, the stones forget their source outside the vortex, where basalt is ubiquitous: singularly the most abundant volcanic rock on the planet (as well as on the Moon, Mars, and Venus). It underlies most of the Earth's surface and ocean floors: in mines, quarries, gravel pits, statues, tombs, grinding pots, thrones, cobblestones, ballasts, tools, pedestals, temples, amphitheaters, archways, columns, earthworks, and meteorites.

Key to the site are mirth and theater: the gesture is ridiculous; an irrational impropriety; an unreasonable imposition on the landscape: incongruous in its place but too precisely logical in its mathematics; overstated and underwhelming; begging for scale because no matter where one stands it always seems both far too small and much too big. The seriousness of its stones rotates to simulate a gravity from which the gleeful whimsy of its form cannot escape — a dark anchor in a crimson lake: *gaiete* [Middle French: jet]; *gaieté* [Modern French: mirth, buoyancy, caprice] — the sinking and the floated. The one mirrors the other, the lake waters reflect the rock. Quarries claster. Mouthy hounds continue to hunt. Sounds evaporate in the desert vast. The sky, reflected, holds the stones aloft. Gravity cancels waft, and queries. But the questions mirrors ask always fall short of the answers they are able to give. Mirrors thrive on surds, and generate incapacity. The larger stones convey the sense of a convoy: an armed escort of the promontory guarding the expeditionary invasion of the lake with a show of lithic force.

Discrepancies of temperature announce themselves with the whole procession and cavalcade: storm, vortex, swarm, serpentage.

The desert adores the unadorned, but spangles diamondbacks.

Duration, since it is not absolute, cannot be measured by the ticks of clocks or metronomes; their hearers are deluded by the incremental.

History and chronology collapse in a hall of mirrors: the pier ("a structure supporting the span of a bridge") is of uncertain origin, in evidence from the postclassical Latin *pera,* which appears to be a variant of *piere* (a building stone, a rock, a precious gem), from the Latin *petra* [stone, rock], but the Latin word derives from the English: in their earliest recorded instance both versions occur in the same manuscript, the Latin preceding the English, textually, but the English preceding the Latin, etymologically, though neither seems to have been derived directly from the other, with internal evidence indicating that the Latin version goes back to an earlier English original, which now is lost, glossed with a belated redundancy on its first appearance. Raising the reflex of more modern English, the word takes the form of *pyre*: a structure for the igneous [from Latin *ignis*: fire].

Resting on a bed of burning basal sands, the basalt, in its blackness, was already jetty ["of the color of jet; jet black," as of cinders], if not yet arrayed into a jutting pier with its absurd incursion into the waters of Great Salt Lake.

Ab + surdus: a number that cannot be expressed in finite terms; irrational; voiceless, "breathed" as opposed to sonant; deaf. The second and third letters of the root of the verb are the same, coalescing to drown out the radical: ally, apprehend, deepen, doom, feel, fool, loom, loop.

Sheets, papers, or cards having edges cut away to facilitate indexing, such as thumb cuts on books, paper cuts to the whorls of the prints on pads — indenting, in every case, interrupts identity — let letters lie open to convey a right; a detailed description of a preferred embodiment follows. Even our history seems at times like a story recorded in a book; some of pieces of each page are missing, providing an indexed codex such as a dictionary, divided up into different alphabetical sections, the pages of each section having a cut-out for viewing the initial letter of all the words in that section and an elongate slot above which is printed the second and third letters of the words printed on that page. The height of the slots is arranged so that the second and third letters printed on one page appear just below the upper edge of the slot in the previous page. With multiple signatures in a system, those with the same second and third letter reveal, through gravimetrics, that cosmic signatures respawn.

Entropy renders every action pyrrhic.

In drops the toxin drips; with ticks and tocks the watches mind; the mined collapses.

Bertram blooms among the croppings, corrupting the fire of the sun.

A contour map rings its perigee with a pressure-drop geometry.

Intensity changes correlate only very weakly with size, but cyclones of the most extreme intensity must be small, tending to develop into more intense hurricanes since the surface dissipation of kinetic energy is restricted to a confined area; high winds are most likely to reach their maximum potential intensity only when compacted.

Cascabels bask on basalt. The monotone tune soon announces the fight: rattle before strike, hiss before panic, coil then assault.

A bellicose slapping tracks the wind speed by the rigging.

Weeds ring the stockade of rocks that once waded the lake.

Black tourmaline, ash-drawing as the magic Sri Lankan lapidary with its massive, compact and columnar, shrunken brittle crystals of complex silicoborate with vitreous lustre, shatters to shrapnel shards from the slightest knapping.

The Catherine wheel tortures as it turns. The sutra serves as torma for the sacrifice.

The scum of the lake laces the slake when the waters withdraw in their slurry of salt.

The typhoon, approaching, churns with slow hurry.

High clouds funnel. The winds raise a wayment, keening. The grasses duplicate the key, mimicking, perfectly, a sigh. Mist from the rushes dissipates. The eye stares, unblinking, in amazement.

An unseen hurricane of carnage functions as the shadow of a shadow, visible only in the ghostly remains of the victims of spectacular time, buried beneath commercial advertising: resutured scalps; maxillary removals; the dehiscence of dorsal surgical incisions displaying right through to the spine before dissolving to a shapeless delirium.

The rain is not the only dash between the earth and sky.

The whirling course of certain meteors were first named κύκλωμα because they recalled the coiling of a snake: nebular serpents of storm and paralysis, with curling arms of clouds armed with isobar fangs, threatening. At some point, the μ mysteriously transformed into an ν, in English orthography merely losing a minim, and recalling the intentional error James Joyce attempted to insert in *Ulysses* in order to transform *Mother* into the telegraphed "Nother" ["another," or "not her"]. French typesetters thought they had corrected yet another obvious misprint from the astigmatic author, but a man of genius makes no mistakes; his errors are volitional and are the portals of discovery.

In Morse Code the difference is only a dot for a dash. In French it works like a midsummer night's dream to transform the soul into an ass, *une âme* for *un âne*. In *Pinocchio,* the puppet, animate but without a soul, and transformed into a donkey, is trapped for a trap and threatened with skinning, after a brine bath; the ringmaster threatens to flay him to make a circus drum. François Rabelais faced a similar fate for the same transformation, although he professed the error, unlike Joyce's, to have been unintentional; on reviewing the serpenting script of his foul papers he found in it not a single doubtful passage, and expressed horror at the foul snake-eater who had brought some charge of moral heresy against him, based solely on a printer's careless, lazy substitution of an n for an m. The same minimal difference accounts for the discrepancy between a house and a gift [*domum, donum*], a trumpeter and a crow [*cornicen, cornicem*], those (who vanquish by the elm), in Limousin, for pimping [*limociniat, lenociniat*].

In lapidary mathematics, where all of the faces either intersect one or more of the axes, or would intersect them if sufficiently extended in each direction, in the determination of the parameters of planes with parallel intersections, the equations of analytical geometry are monometrically simplified if we can substitute m for n.

The fraught etymology of *Tassinong,* shrouded in obscurity, attests to the same danger, unable to distinguish between bad French and Algonquian. One source suggests the subsidence of rocks into the soft silt of the lakebed with a sinking or settling, as stones plumb in mud. Another raises stockades from berry thickets, imprisoning history. The locative may simply have indicated an area without any landmarks or monuments.

Pictarne storm as the terns and petrels migrate back for summer. Stunted mountain juniper attract the mistle-thrush above the columbine and thistle. The nosecones of jet-engines sport signature spirals. The targeted missile rushes but misses. The payloads plummet. The taxiway at the Proving Grounds below the lake is three times the length of the *Jetty*; the runway over seven times. In 1968, some agent from a Skyhawk drifted from the base, mixing with the rain and snow that swept across the plains below; the Skull Valley sheep kill left six thousand animals dead.

In the tarpaper darkness of a shack, not far from shore, a lone hole allows a slight cone of light in which motes swirl in curling air currents before winking out as others appear in the blizzard of disturbance. Beneath the porch shelter serpents.

The snake winds; the watch-case nacres; the mind relapses.

Smithson saw the Guggenheim museum as Frank Lloyd Wright's most visceral achievement: an inverse digestive tract of ambulatories metaphorized as intestines, a waste system that had taken architectural form.

As if the momentous coil of the intestines had risen to the surface of the greater omentum by virtue of the convulsive struggle of their excremental toil in its scatologic task, or had been mimicked by the circular stercorary decoration of fecal insignia copying the unique cropped device of some Regent of Helicology with anticipatory plagiarism, Jarry inscribed the swollen belly of his coprolalic King Ubu — few met a more euphoric, admired, participatory panegyrist to dejection, though thinking no small beer of himself, self-absorbed with a complacent, profitless expenditure that comes from believing one's the sun around which common planets revolve, the center of his universe, waving his arms from their honor, fess and nombril, wagging his emphatic phallus, from Cusco to Delphi, Kailash to Easter Island, obliging otherwise decent, honest umpires to concede his achievements though even the humble man on the Clapham omnibus can see the conceited cockerel has no clothes — with the circling rings of an algorithmic spiral. Like a ditched wheel above a beautiful workshop gutter or usine sewer, spinning uselessly without advance, this ubique iconography, encountered everywhere in nature, and even in the prolonged utopia parkway of annulled parts, was named *la gidouille.*

It might suggest both the word and meaning of *andouille,* "a big hogges gut stuffed with small guts (and other intrailes)," and remembering Ubu's propensity to outbursts, exclamations, and ejaculations we might note that the word contains an expressive, affirmative cry of pain (*ouille!*), or perhaps a garbled, indigestive version of the medieval French *gargouille* (to gurgle) — the very source of *jargon* itself; but Jarry had learned another word from reading François Rabelais: *guédouille,* an oil container with a double reservoir and helicated neck-spouts that twist like swans in love, or like a sebaceous set of sacks in testicular torsion.

Accordingly, if Ubu were aggrandized so his *gidouille* were congruent with the *Spiral Jetty,* his umbilicus would hold a volume just equal to the lower limit defining a "large spill" of crude oil, or the oil that gurgled to the surface one day in June, along an Allegheny tributary, birthing the Seneca Oil Company, which would have displaced the amount of regular unleaded gasoline overflowing the top of a tank in Rogers, Arkansas, at the Morgan Stanley well 141 years later, which was double the engine displacements of the tainted vehicles Volkswagen conceded it would buy back after its fraudulent emissions scandal, or the per-household vehicle-fuel consumption of gasoline in the United States in the late '80s, the same amount furnished to the Senate garage by the Texas Company in one month (July, 1932, at 7.39 cents per gallon, still just a hair under $1.33 generally at today's rate, although actually a negative $107.92 dollars in late April, 2020), the output of a single Tehran refinery during the War of the Cities, equal to the kerosene issued to the U.S. military as it fought at Wounded Knee or the fuel oil discharged to shore-docks at Dungarvan in 1923, or the seal oil procured one summer at Quoin Rock (west of Cape Agulhas), as the surf thundered above the cry of gulls, or the whale oil wrung by crofter fishermen, with makeshift means, on Orkney and sold at Newcastle, as George Low made his surveying tour of the island, or the cocoanut oil floated by ship from Nicobars to Calcutta along with 16,627 seamen, and the amount of "pure olive oil" (really cottonseed oil) exported from New York to England for Queen Victoria's Diamond Jubilee, the linseed oil from New Orleans as streetcar service expanded past Napoleon Avenue and from Philadelphia to Messrs. McCulloch & Alexander in Edinburgh a century earlier, the winter oil wangled by the City of Philadelphia from Diehl & Duff as the Christiana Riot trials began at $1.20 per gallon (less one cent per gallon for casks returned), the benzine accounted for in the costs of the Picton government as it established the first residential institution for child migrants, the specific amount of turpentine gum hawked as Apollo 13 launched toward the moon, the cartons of copper preservative conceded to Tilapia fisheries in British Guiana as the Church of England lends its moral backing to family planning, the bright varnish gamed by the U.S. Navy in Singapore as catfish fell from the skies, the No. 61 drier measure dispensed in Pratt & Lambert paints from their plant in Long Island City as the five boroughs of greater New York consolidated, the increase in the amount of Fluid Extracts and Tinctures manufactured by the New York Department of Hospitals as Berenice Abbott swept back into town, or the creosote expended per saturation load of telegraph-pole preparation by S.B. Boulton's Patent Process (good for a full forty-seven poles, enough to cover a mile of open western ground).

Une gibbe denotes a kind of "coquille terrestre, univalve [univalve land snail]" as Émile Littré has it, with its distinctive spiral shell and its ommatophores just visible in the geminate *b* of the word itself, rising like the double-necked flasks of a *guédouille*.

At the same time, vintners use *ouiller* to describe the act of periodically topping off a wine cask during the first days of fermentation so that evaporation and the extravasation of the yeasty foam of dregs leave no space for oxidation. Accordingly, at the center of his jutting, paunchy dome—bloated taut with feasting on biscuits soggy with jelly and corned beef hash topped with eggs — Ubu's *Jetty* bellybutton could hold, instead of petrochemicals: a lasht of hops (the dry product unit of measure used in Baltic ports from the fourteenth to nineteenth centuries); the mash in store at Mr. Cornelius Quigg's still in Philadelphia when inspected for fraud as the Albany Bachelor Baseball Club travels to confront the Excelsior and Pythians at the Parade Grounds; the vat of strong ale brewed for the Marquis of Abercorn, Dublin (along with some light ale of a very indifferent quality, though perhaps too strong, meted to his sopped servants, in order to forfend a palace coup) as a semaphore line is stretched across the Irish Sea; the amount of strong beer dispersed to the populace of Salisbury, as Constable paints the cathedral from Bishop Fisher's garden, as ordered by the Mayor; the carriage of strong beer imported as the first of the Springhill Mining Disasters struck into Cannington, Wapella, and Moosomin; barrels seized and staved for unlicensed brewing in West Clive as the Fourth Street funicular's White Line opens in Dubuque; the Beere kept in the cellar according the probate inventories of the Wellington mercers; an amount taken to the cellar as Rinaldo and Almirena celebrate their love among the rebuke of the poisoning arts of Adulteratings, Sophistications, and corrupt Mixtures; the yield of hard cider from an acre of Red-Strakes and Golden Pippins; the light wine meant to sustain a crew of thirty-nine men over a five-month period while whaling off Honfleur during which Blaise Pascal's *Lettres provinciales* are shredded and burnt; the wine drunk daily among the furs and pleasures and sparkling jewels at the most memorable and honorable incident of Kenilworth Castle during the Royal entertainment by the Earl to his Queen; the equal amounts of Verzenay, Ay, Cramant, and Avize, respectively, in the coupage of cuvée in the fine years 1857 and 1858, or of Bouzy, Pierry, Cramant, and Avize, respectively, in another; the wine ruined by inferior grapes injured by rain at Verzenay; the bottles purveyed by Theobald le Botiller at Dublin as John Rogers Thomas composes "The Rose of Killarney"; tintos and brancos imported by Strobel and Church, to Liverpool from Portugal, despite the Siege of Almeida; the Bordeaux brought to London by the merchant Adventurers mixed up with the Pilgrims as the *Mayflower* prepares to sail; the magnums stowed by George DuBois for his voyage aboard the *Titanic*; the tankards brought to Portsmouth from Oporto on the *Betty* as John assumes Most Faithful Majesty; the rum transferred from the Sloop *Betsey* to the Sloop *Liberty* by Dr. Foushee, run on the *Lydia* from the West Indies to Nova Scotia, imported with promissory note, written in a fine Spencerian hand, by the subscriber, Christopher Leffingwell, to the colony of Connecticut from Granada on the Brig *Brittania,* or sold by J. Cameron to G. Knight at twenty-six days' credit in March of 1850 — a weight for which the stevedores at Demerara charged eight cents in the summer, a half-century later.

For that fee they would have carried: the spirits stored in the old Commissary department in Bethlehem after the resignation of Quartermaster Mifflin; the volume of intoxicating liquors seized by the Marshal in Lewiston, Maine, some sixteen years prior; which matched the volume of Hesperidina ushered into Bilbao from Argentina, where the first recorded tango, Angel Vollod's "El Choclo," was all the rage; or the volume of malt spirits distilled in Scotland the year a meteorite fell on the North Inch at Perth; or the full stores of spirits equipped, obtained in a pinch by feat of force, by the expeditionary detachment of the Russian Army in its advance to Khiva; which was the same as all the substandard alcohol exposed by sanitary inspectors in Russia during the Russo-Georgian War; or the export of ethyl alcohol from potatoes by Danish factory De Danske Spiritfabrikker as suicides in Denmark are studied according to social status and sex.

The same magnitude of apple brandy, undissipated, led to a disputed case in the federal appeals courts; an equal dram of rum, in corked kegs, was at issue in the cause of action litigated between Orme and Keigwin and James Henry Parry; the sugar at issue in the suit drummed dramatically between Rhode and Thwaites, Allen and Hodge, and lodged between Lambeth and

Joffrion, averaged the production of the most important plantation estate in Jamaica as it abolishes slavery, or of the low and swampy Levy on the Florida peninsula, equaling cargo taken on by the U.S.S. *Rattler* at Chamberlain's plantation in Louisiana and delivered to the prize steamer *Elmira*, or the fraight in Hall for which was rendered many harty thankes by William Berkeley.

That bulk equaled the crates of darkly black and adulterated "old tobacco" packed to Dundee from the Clyde, seized as *honesta spolia* by General Blakeney from the custom-house in Alloa, Clackmannanshire, during the rebellion of 1745, or bound, with the same stemmed press of dried and candied leaves as browned and tacky pages — their leather edges curling from the curing — in volumes of a circulating nightshade library of inscribed alkaloids, disseminating a parasympathomimetic stimulation of the nicotinic muscarine but printed at an unredeemable cost of captive blood, for Bristol a century earlier, discounted by the creditor Major Theophylus Hone as allowing for being the most part of it rotten on arrival or just a decade earlier discovered in a probate home, aged and unaccounted for in a cellar, lodged without clearance, a cargo which John Fuller received two years later, in acrimonious negotiation with his son, Rose, held inaccessibly close in the hull as the *Success* of Ayr cleared out for Norway, shipped by Robert Wormeley Carter of Sabine Hall, to England, the same sad mean stuff shipped to Holland on the *Brilliant* and again imported by Hamilton and Company from America, then to Malta, via Rotterdam, to France for commercial purposes via Leghorn, then picked up at the mouth of the Elkhorn by the *Falls City* steamer around about 1907, with the bill of lading hidden under a lantern, which would have brought an average of seven dollars and twenty cents on the market, which was the weak weekly tobacco sales at Louisville forty years earlier, the very amount disputed in the lawsuit that arose from an Internal Revenue seizure, contested in the complaint about freight rates from Paris to New Orleans on the Chattanooga line by Douthitt and Crossway a half-dozen years on, and a decade later the full load in a thirty-six-foot car given the standardization of casks sought by the railroad interests, equivalent to 19,300,800 cigarettes, enough to keep the average Andorran smoking for 1,610 years, the average Czech away from the *trafika* for 4,242 years, *le citoyen moyen en tabagisme pour 9,450 ans,* and contented the average placid island inhabitant of the Abode of Peace for over a million years, or one cigarette for everyone in Jakarta, or Lima, or Nagoya, or Bangkok, or almost every denizen of Wuhan, or a pack for every resident of Sacramento, California.

In a metempsychotic transmigration of volume through various bodies, the soul of this khoric form would find itself stamped out into the materials of like liquids and fungible solids in translation, fraught, or funded in stock—the single volume metamorphosing in slow retards and sudden streaking rushes taking a myriad of contained shapes as it finds itself relaxed or constricted, a collapse of relative scales that one can compress or expand indefinitely as long as they share a common reference, a transposition of several diverse bodies but all the same volume, every time seeking its own level: the powder cached in a Celler in London to sett on fyre on the night of an anti-royalist uprising in 1666; the bread packed from a Baiker in Perth, bought by one of the Jacobite Lairds of Gask in 1746; the casks of loose skins brought by Pococke in March, 1768, on the *Lloyd* out of Charleston from plantations to Bristol; the amount of water to which one of the crystals, only as large as a pinpoint, will give a distinguishable green hue when heated to nearing the same degrees; the stock, on the victualling ship *Planter,* of pease provisioned in 1797 for the magazine of Admiral Nelson's fleet in ration to its crew; the neat herring over clearance lardered on the *Gunnie May* in 1887; the entrepot of staves purchased from a cooper with monies given in order to construct the Lotus-Eater style of a Colonial Scheme Divan and Cozy Corner curtained with care by a mesh of crêpe; in the ambry of the brig-sloop *L'Aimable Henriette,* the caskets of coffee invoiced to Bordeaux from Port-au-Prince one January in the 19th century; such pouring salt abated to from 250 tons, sent by Mr. Onge, from

Lisbon on a fated Dutch ship; the price of a musket in the South China Sea when filled full of foot-long bêche-de-mer.

The miners strike a deal; the snake oils; the tics slacken.

At the same time, *douillage* connotes defective or shoddy manufacture, especially of textile fabrics, from irregular quality (as when different materials are worked into the weft, or different sources or spare parts are grafted together).

Une douille, on the other hand, is the hollow cylindrical socket into which something is fitted (as a bayonet or spade to a barrel or haft), suggesting perhaps the threaded hollow waiting to receive a sexual or violent thrust. The *gidouille* of Ubu Roi might be a sort of inverted corkscrew—a device not for opening a bottle but for siphoning a funneled libation *into* the king.

However such vessels might communicate, or the ambiguous coupling of the ducts conduct their conveyance, the sixteen-and-nine-tenths hogshead of his umbilicus could accommodate all of the soup distributed by the Kensington Soup Society Soup House during the 1995–96 year, or the aggregate milk output of Israeli dairies in 1933, which equaled the average annual milk from the udder of a single Ayrshire-breed heifer in 1948 (the record set in 1920 by Dunlop Treasure produced the same amount in forty-six weeks), or the daily sales of the Mahasang's Mahananda cooperative dairy from their sacred herd in 1987.

The form, in fact, flows through time: pouring, imperceptibly, over centuries, as even the same substance—*pli selon pli*—recurs in its slow, seeping, eternal sentry relief of shift into shift without seizing from pale dawn of each decade's day to the darkness secured at unconscionable cost. The crystals melt into silky refinement. The third boil raises a caramel musk. Five thousand times more viscous than bovine milk, and still one hundred times more viscous than the oil in a *guedoufle,* the slow, thick flow of unsulfured, blackstrap molasses—reluctant to take leave of the bordering, sloped sides of a jetty-center-sized umbilicus — would equal the amount seeping like a sucrose mnemonic between the *Concord,* bound for Virginia from Barbados, without the gold dust and ivory deemed too valuable to risk and a century later, to the varied conmixture procured by Peleg Green for Aaron Lopez from St. Anns, the island that autumn being only indeferent in the Molasses way, to 1813 when the insured amount was found burnt in a Schooner to 1824 when the discrepancy between the claims shipped and received from Haiti to the United States was noted to two decades later when the exact same *part maudite* was lost between what the despairing Sheriff made, for real, and what he accounted, in deceit, the same disparity the very year in the past yield revised downward by the overseer on a Jamaica plantation due to slave revolt, equaling twelve aspents of Creole cane, half a century later in paid receipt for twenty-one bales of middling upland cotton supposedly sold by a commission merchant, half-a-dozen years on the good heavy syrup from ten acres, next year the yield of cold measure semi-sirup mashed from a field of sorghum cane, to 1887 and the imported total by the farmers of Liberty County, Texas, two years later, and a dozen years later to the import, valued at $192, by the Philippine Islands from the United States and a half-dozen on again to the rate per acre of tricresol solution received by a check plat of Rayada cane in a two-year experimental span of lipophilic antioxidant wash and root-soak preservative.

Those sugary syrups could have been washed down with a bellyful reservoir holding exactly the amount of water dropped on Puerto Rico by the Okeechobee hurricane, provoking the first storm warning broadcast by radio and putting an end to the island's coffee industry, a measure that would pass in one minute through the record-setting Seagrave model multi-stage centrifugal pump set to 132 pounds pressure in the exhibition at New Orleans, equal to the Mississippi River water pumped per pound of equivalent coal by Allis-Chalmers Vertical Compound Engines from the 1890s and two 1912 DeLaval Twin Centrifugal steam turbine-driven engines, with low voltage fluctuations, at

Chain of Rocks station in St. Louis, where the slope of the channel drives the water along the talweg to over six feet per second, which equals the irrigation per apple tree using conventional non-drip systems, or the amount of condensed water that must be had at a cost of one pound sterling before it pays to use a condenser, or the amount wasted if a faucet runs a "thread" of water one-half-inch long before it begins to form drops.

The same sum of water was purchased by a floating army dredge plant just before the outbreak of the First World War, which was equal to the average daily consumption of Loretto borough, Pennsylvania, at the time of the death of Charles Schwab, who led Bethlehem Steel to become the second largest manufacturer in the United States, and whose estate soon supplied water to the town from its two wells, which held the capacity of the covered wooden coagulating basins into which centrifugal pumps, powered by an 80-horsepower gas-fired Erie boiler, discharge after mixing, through very crude devices, alum and soda ash, via wrought-iron suction pipes, the turbid waters of the Monongahela one-and-one quarter miles above the mouth of Deckers creek to supply Morgantown, an aggregate capacity of the six storage tanks on the facilities property of the Metropolitan Telecommunications Corporation in Toledo, disclosed in their listing application to the American Stock Exchange, or the larger of two reservoirs on the hill above Le Raysville, Pennsylvania, as the U.S. Open was held in Gladwyne, to serve a population of 298 (steadily dropping, one person per decade, over the next seventy years), or the cistern at Number Sixteen Broad Street sold on account of James Stewart's health and his intention to remove to his country house, on Bloomingdale Road, as permanent retirement abode. Each of which was exactly the minimum capacity of the emergency diesel generator at Prairie Island Nuclear Generating Plant in Redwing, Minnesota, on the floodplain of the Mississippi, or the old 1946-style system converted into a Doyle patented "fast-cycle" compressed-air evacuator two decades later, or the settling compartment of the Imhoff tank at the treatment plant constructed in Winchester,

Virginia, as Winona was platted in Norfolk, which takes about two hours to filter the wastes from the woolen mills that mix with the city sewage, slightly faster than the two-and-one-half hours it takes to lose the same amount of liquid in stand-pipe while pumping during hot weather, in the latter part of May and first part of June in South Weymouth, Massachusetts, as the first World Series was set to be played in Boston, an amount raised 54 yards, per hour, by the steam engine at Doonan, or the same mass raised ten feet by one-hundred-men force by Mr. Blakey's patented steam engine, the ballooning, peak daily water quality change of sewage estimated from the Big Wood Ski Area development in the Sawtooth National Forest, the amount of Leicester effluents treated in seventy-eight hours to remove over 200,000 strands of agar bacteria (at 37° Celsius) as the Grand Hotel is built in Granby Street, though it would take only a day to pump using a Worthington compound duplex machine, by which time the same flow would have passed through the dump tank in Exeter (Belle Isle) as the new, stronger, flatter cast-iron bridge was opened when a rope stretched across the roadway was ceremonially cut by the Mayor Councillor.

Indeed, the gargantuan umbilical cavity would be filled to its ridge by the weekly fecal output of the Lancaster elementary school district as the Battle of Los Angeles raged, or of the youth population of Harlow thirty years later — or by the hebdomadal flux of the Spanish Sahara (as its conquest was at last completed at the end of the 19th century), or Mahatpur, Nadiya, Bengal, at the founding of the Indian League, Peñaranda, Philippines, at the time it was ceded to the United States by Spain, Cattaro, a fortified Austrian port on the Dalmatian coast, during the First World War, or the town of Dinuba in the San Joaquin valley during the Second World War; the same feculence would pack the cavity of Ubu's umbilicus with the weekly defecations of the populace of either Mola, Naples, or Giesse, Hesse-Darmstadt, as the King of the Two Sicilies sailed for Madrid, or the eight villages of Lathi, India, or Marala, Pakistan during the war with India, where the new mandi had sprung up near the railway station, equal to the seven-day's voiding of Norman, Minnesota, or Santa Cruz del Quiché, Guatemala at the turn of the millennium, the population of Привілля (Ukraine), or Privais, the small capital of the department Aedèche as Gérard de Nerval commits suicide, or Bromberg, Prussia, as Bismarck takes control, which would balance the evacuations made in a week on Charlotte Amalie, on St. Thomas in 1924, San Marino, Italy, in 1865, or St. Helena (British territory) in 2012, a congruence of Charlton and Jasper Counties (Georgia), or Sitka Borough with Florence in 1994 and Mojave County thirty years earlier, Jackson County in 1974 and LaFayette County (Arkansas) eighty years earlier, Oregon City at the falls of the Willamette in 1952 and Bend a quarter-century earlier, displacing the same weekly discharges from Smiths Falls, Ontario in 1947, Corte Madera, California, two decades later, and everyone living in the greater Reykjavik area by the following decade. The catastrophic rain of dirty, semisolid waste in the tens of thousands of turds dropped over seven days in Sharkey County, Missouri, another decade on, or Makushi, Guyana, another decade later still would fill the pit at the center of the *gidouille* as would the basins emptied from Schönheide, Erzgeb, Germany, in 1910. From Gainesville, Texas, a decade later to Brantly County, Georgia, a decade later still, the same swill exudes. These hebdomadary excremental discharges would be met by Lancaster, Pennsylvania, as Moyamensing Prison opened, Wagga Wagga, Australia, during the Oombulgurri massacre, Dickenson, Virginia, as work was begun on the Panama Canal, Fostoria, Ohio, as the Great White Fleet set out to circumnavigate the globe, Tucker County, West Virginia, as Jacques Picard descends into the Mariana Trench in the Bathyscaphe *Trieste,* or Plainfield, New Hampshire, as utilities in Flint, Michigan, begin to source their water from the local river … all equivalent to the feces shit in a humid week by the human inhabitants of the island of Ofu, American Samoa, in 1991, the non-indigenous population in Indonesia in 1828, the white population in Harlem in 1910, the men in Karabük, Anatolia, early in the Cold War, the Catholics in Katunayake, Sri Lanka, in 1990, or the deaf population of New Zealand in 2011.

The snake cases its prey; the watch chain rattles; miners relax.

Although the edematous Ubu, degenerate, would complete the task with greater alacrity and lusty dipsetic dispatch — not to mention an abundance of easily discerned albuginous depositions scaling the tank as they sank to the sloping cistern walls of the caldera, salted by sediment with gentle settling care — and assuming hydration in keeping with the arid climate of the Great Basin, it would take eight years and eight long mictural months, the full wartime period of the Continental Army, or the time it took for Islam to reach the rocky fastness of Asturias after the victory of the Moors, or to bore the St. Gothard tunnel on Rail Route Ten through the petrifact Tyrol mountains, for the average person, astrangurious and free from ischuria, to fill the navel of the spiral *gidouille* by passing — with daily, regular staling — over the precipice of its isthmian fold, a dazzling cataract, all the more scintillating in the desert sun, as the steaming stream cascades with the tintinnabulary chime of calming chamber music when it meets the turgid, tetrapyrrolic pond of settling solids. By the time the Army stood down there would be in the lotium an accumulation of some 188 kilograms of urea and various dry and volatile sediments filtering in suspended fall beneath the epistasis swirling in a spiraled nebular float of sodium lotion like some vast gassy galaxy bathing in the glassy golden glow of a hundred billion suns to a clouded amber depth, the nepheloid sublation cradling the weight of the second lactation of a flock of Cagliari sheep, the seeding of an hectare of fava beans in China, or the ethyl alcohol from a ton of corn residue, or taken together: a diuretic diet evoking an emulsified Sardinian memory of summer legumes simmered in wine and served with shavings of pecorino, cracked peppercorns, and a first-press drizzle of deep golden olive oil — enough to feed an army — before the vast vespasienne, taxing the atmosphere with the passing of blistering, foul ammoniacal fumes — keen, eye-watering to a caustic chemical burn — crystallizes in the sun to gleam like some precious omphacitic stone, mutragalactic, as rare as the ligure that the ancients believed to be concretized from the urine of lynxes, who themselves know of the conversion, and because of their jealous nature, they protect, as much as they are able, their fluid discharge in desert places.

The amount of breast milk suckled by 360 infants, nursed until they utter their first words, would, mingling in the leats of wrinkled channels from pannicular folds, also fill the trough, as would a single mother's leaking teats with a lactating seep lasting, assuming agogic circadian rhythms, eleven years and some eight months: the minimum degree of *cadena perpetua* in force in the Philippines according to the penal code at the time of the Tagalog Insurgency.

Assuming neither allergies nor viral infections, seven-and-one-half mucilaginous years of productive expectoration from the trachea, bronchia, and lungs would pass in trooping, steady march of attenuating meldrops and impelled drips to pool a pituitous, transparent lake of remarkable viscidity yet capable of being drawn out into strings as fine as melted glass and stretching back to match the wick of a lamp — a blennorrhagic consistency with little annual variation, neither thickened by the winter cold nor coagulated by the summer heat, which would lead to little or no caking from desiccation nor skin to skim or peel, from the surface, blistering (Ubu, sniveling, would sooner be swimming in the lip-level phlegm of the umbilical lake).

The same space would be filled by the saliva produced in twenty-one years, although glutinous Ubu, sybaritic, *in flagrant delict,* would slaver the pit at a quicker pace with his incessant thoughts of elaborate blanketed victuallage picnics, *fêtes champêtres,* pageanted banquets, and profane comessation to statuvalent stupor without crapulous fast.

The pool would brim, additionally, with the perspiration from twenty-three eccrinous and apocrinous weeks of continuous, vigorous exercise — an hebdomadal exudation that would shed 441.5 adipose pounds from the morbidly obese gymnast: the daily caloric requirement of an average adult Blue Whale; the annual per-capita consumption of humans (including some needed animal feed and industrial crops such as cotton), requiring an arable hectare for every thirty or forty people, an amount saved by increased use of rotation of winter-cover crops of legumes, which fixes the nitrogen as green manure, compared to the use of commercial fertilizers, equal to the yield of one acre of wheat; the heat needed to dry and fire one thousand bricks, requiring two to three hundred kilograms of bituminous coal, generating enough energy to power a fodder cutter through one hundred pounds of dried hay feed, to harvest one hundred bushels of grain, to prepare an average electric oven-cooked meal, equal to the rate increase of residential consumer utility consumption in Minneapolis in August, 1932, the lowest consumption of frozen-food-locker plants operating in Illinois just before the Second World War, an energy required to move a one-man street car one mile along the Sunset line in El Paso during the First World War, or the same car-mile of an elevator running at full speed a half mile up and down, without any stops, or the energy needed to lift one acre-foot of water a height of one foot, or one hundred kilograms from the surface of the earth and all the way to infinity.

The blind orifice would accommodate the secretions of cyprine from 3,506 celibate years exuded without arousal or manual stimulation.

Or, in the time it takes the Gregorian calendar to acquire one too many days to keep pace with the hurl of the earth around its solar pole—*id est,* 3,320 years: from the reign of gallant Menes to the days of Herodotus, the prison sentence of each Rote Hilfe Deutschlands worker arrested by the Gestapo in 1935, or the time it takes to double the South Korean population, or the period of the occlusion of Arabia Petraea from European knowledge—the slow lachrymal fountains of eyes untroubled by keratoconjunctivitis sicca, not blinking overmuch from erratic saccades, nor caring for overlong stelling or staring, nor beset by the winds, both arent and arenose, would brim the telluric depression with their natural tearing, a fill even faster afforded with deploring, bealing to raise wind-bells in water, shriking or squinnying, watercarted, or in any way crying, sobbing, or weeping from weak autonomic limbic response.

Or then, again, with attendant chafing and chapping, the once immaculate canyon could also be filled by deliriously well over a million ejaculations.

The watch-chain snakes; the fangs lock; the miners clock long hours.

Fossilated specimens dominate the Carboniferous. They towered as forests, far beyond their roots, with a verdant canopy covering the land that remained above rising seas. As the biomass compacted over the surface of the earth at its maximum density — spooring through the sponge of loam, floating on the stagnant surface of the swampy waters — the Kingdom of the plants, unable to expand, struck upward, colonizing the air with a vertical foison, vying with flying insects in a photosynthesis of three-dimensional space. The foliating profusion, with a monticulous rash of buds erupting over vascular skin, deciduating torrents, and a steady pollinating rain, supplied so much oxygen that arthropods could grow to monstrous sizes, concomitant with the sudden new surge of flora — arthropleura on the rainforest floors churned the viscous brack, a quiver of ribs in scurry from scorpions the size of leopard sharks; meganeura as big as seagulls thrummed with a deafening oscillation, vibrating the carapaces of archimylacrids like thorax-clappered bells, ringing the changes across a scurrying carillon that swarmed with alacrity in a clattering peal — and everything scorched in the superoxygenated atmosphere. Even the tropical swamps were flammable under such conditions — the logged and swollen plants at risk of the very fires that they made possible with their stomatic respiration. Every forest fire then enriched the slurried soil, in turn, spurring new growth in a cultivation of light-gathering, incendiary fuel, reflecting back in miniature the solar flares that they digested. The phoenix arboretum of Pangea cycled for centuries in suicidal immolations; its coal forests of lycopsids, rising like hundred-foot club mosses, and arborescing lepidodendrals looming skyward—their scaly trunks snapping in the rush of winds that followed the vacuum suck of combustion in the firestorms that ruddled the infernal skies—have long ago collapsed, but fern species survived, diminishing through the centuries from tree-size down, in slow arboreal demise, to rhizomatic ground cover.

The lace of pinnulets in spray from blades filters the midday light. Fiddleheads in autumn spiral through the undergrowth. Their tight fists, like a newborn's fingers, clench the shadows of the shade along the edge of forest glades and hold fast the cool, which it preserves, as morning dissipates.

A lintie chittles in the canopy.

The frond uncoils, the bindweed shrinks, the bud escapes the cap-pinched clutch to which it was consigned, the seed projects, the branches reach, the palmate towers like a trophy, the primrose fades to sparks, the faint prints of the sandalled foot of nature traces paths upon the flora of the park with a trimmed, embroidered dance. The botanical foils the plans of the gardener. Toeprints dimple the soil in fans of frozen sprays; the heel-strike marks the rhythm of a strophe. After, the darkness dims from dusk. The pattern passes out of sight.

A web is fed through a leaf of heddles on a shaft, separating warp threads into tunnels through which the weft shuttle easily passes. The weave of pinnae in the breezes lofts like fairy fingers petting their familiar shadows with a barely felt caress. Sucrose fetters later growth but spurs the first fissure of a cytokinesis. Cells soak the hormones in patterned concentrations.

The solute potential decreases; the meniscus swells; capillary actions wick; transpiration follows in a mist.

At first, braced by the hardened collar of a petiole, the tightly packed primordia contract to shield pinnae born on rachides; stacked in nascent structures of inflorescent symmetry and taper, they spread outward over time in bialate, dipterous, bilateral spans. The rachis stands against the geotropic pull of the petrose mass from which it ventures. Rain pocks the soil despite the canopy. Ether-extractable auxins predict uncoiling at inviolate rates, measured by degrees of curvature.

The breeze bows the boughs which spring back in ascenting bobs. An accipiter soars in the updraft of a thermal. Crows protest and bluster. Fern seed congeals the blood of the sun, concealing it beneath its leaves in dried drops of solar fire said to shine on the solstice when gathered at midnight, illuminating veins of precious metals hidden in the earth. The passer tressilates at the hum of the sudden sound. Shadows mask occipital blotches confluent from the postocular stripe as they blend to the pattern of scattered black-scale tips. The fluff of cottonwood descends in drifts. Anisoptera dart and pause among the parted fronds, in counterbalanced aerial ballets of drop and lift and hover, alighting in pure water. Their unequal wings shed vortices past bluff bodies into eddies. Ecdysis splits the difference between fern and rattle, the soft, segmented annuli that form the abdomen, pale green from the moult, pulse in mirror to the chitinous articulated taper of the case. The old skin clings to stems and drapes scattered among wilted fern and rose. Degrees of petiolation divide the tribes.

The prehensile tail of a chameleon curls in aggression. Its predatory tongue strikes with deadeye accuracy to twice its body length. Each spirals and extends to maintain an anatomical symmetry. The lizard balances between the pans of spirals and assays the gravitational rate.

Species accept the territorial, but challenge its contours with song.

A sudden rattle panics and adaws.

Botrychium virginianum was thought, across cultures, to be alexiteric. Both the Chippewa and Cherokee applied the masticated plant to bites from rattlesnakes. With an apotropaic structure, the fronds swaylike silent vegetal versions of the violent, terrisonous rattle.

Ferns turn, rhizomatic, on the terraced earth. A single, sterile, sessile leaf spreads above a basal stalk. It shades a snail from oppressive heat. The austere and ascetic sexuality of the botanical is discernible in the circinate vernation of a curled ptyxis. Sunlight swells the solutes of the cells. The water gradient drops and the leaf rises, its volume increasing with a steady tumescence, and then suddenly the bolt and range of succernation assumes its moment of jeté.

With sufficient voltage, fern-like patterns branch across the grassy meadows after lightning strikes. The Lichtenberg figures spread fingers of light-writing in a natural photography of forking paths.

In ribbons of ink-spot droplets sporangia fox in clusters on the verso of the leaf: in a philological assembly draping the shoulders of the fronds that carry them, gatherings of gathering, mentioning in undertones, with whispered hints, and which together, sooth to say, form a sort of folder, file, or sheaf. They will develop through their own spirals in turn, bringing together all the disparate materials that belong together on the topic: a bundle of archival print clippings and manuscripts, bound with a tie of narrow linen fabric — *ein Konvolut.*

Here and there the stalks lean together at some unsustainable height, meeting in an ogival incline — a cathedral in convolution, having the whorls flattened out in the direction of the axis and wound on each other, so as nearly or entirely to conceal the spire.

The stridulating choir, collugent, waxes and swells before falling still.

What pastoral duties does the symbol of this sylvan office signify?

Rubbed, the fronds sate and soothe skin stung by a nettle.

The species rival one another for survival. The fittest mate.

Pannicles, bracts, and sepals protract; the waxy oils of a certate settles; mature fronds fan, bud scales veil the sap. By the end, each chapter captures the very same narrative arc.

Mannered, fatal, indifferent to action, causation, or chronology, with all the legato of a series of present participles circling the indirect silence of some mystic Symbolism, the story is retold in the neo-baroque of the *Jugendstil,* where the florid is no longer the ephemeral perfume of the bloom but its morbid decay and the same delight in the never-ending curve (whether it be growing fern, ammonite, or embryonic curl), the same profusion of minutiae, spurs the deflection of the eye and mind from satiated pleasure, which it defers, with its distractions of unending delight.

The ear perks; the finger prints; the cord twists.

(Soaring steganopods in thrillful aerial parade seek to depatriate the *terre haute* each season.)

In the exaggerated morphology of the Carboniferous we can see, with crisp clarity, the prehistory of the optical unconscious — the stage setting of its dream-world work of enlargement, as if the mere field of the garden yard were magnified to jungle proportions. A *Wundergarten* of architectural forms blooms beneath the focus of the oxygen-clear air. The details they reveal are a vivid reminder of everything not even sensed, or actively repressed, or quickly sublimated by the visual as the brain ventures through the skull with the antennae of the optic nerves, in cautious, blinking proving of the illuminated surround. The primordial view reveals the architecture of botanical anatomy in full focus: ancient fluted columns of horsetails, carved long-house lodge-poles in acorn sprouts, the totem poles of chestnut shoots, the staves of bishops in fern fronds, a teasal's tracery of gothic cathedral window frames, a fin-de-siècle Métro kiosk distributing the news from flowers — all focused at the power objective of ten — so that we discover, from the vantage of that window and the tabloid of the newsstand, not the adaptation of the natural world to decorative ends (the baroque scrollwork of acanthus and floral filigree, the Art Nouveau tendrils of botanical carnivores, the stylized blossoms of Arts & Crafts, or the inbred hothouse orchids of Decadence) but rather nature itself always already in imitation of cultural artifacts and fetishes. The vertiginous mirror inventories perception, recording the heights of artifice in the double-column ledger of the natural, the beauty before the bloom, the pathos of form before the absence of the symbolic.

A lightning flash reveals the two poles of past and future in the dialectical image of the giant fern.

In the ambiguous zone revealed by that profane illumination, a terrain vague of after-image and shadow in which one can no longer distinguish between motion and stillness, time and relation, technology and nature, or recall the difference between the precision of science and the power of magic, or discern the obscene from the occult, the lithic and the living, we can sense the potential energy of the *Spiral Jetty*. If, in some blistering atmosphere predominated by oxygen, in a world returned to the prehistoric with all the vengeance of a patient revolution, a fern were grown to the size of the *Jetty* — or if the ancients were right, and stones are in fact animate and vivid, not the embodiment of the lifeless but merely moving more slowly than we are able to perceive, a floral petrogeny blossoming over eons with the lapidary hatching of spoors — the sculpture might begin to straighten. At the rate of the familiar forest fern, uncanny in its application to the geologic, inducing a dizzying sense of acceleration and vertiginous speed, an unprecedented velocity of rock in motion with a celerity sprung free from its geometric scalentiy, it would take nine and a half days for it to fully uncurl.

In that unfurling, the work would finally achieve its full potential. A jetty, from the French *jeter* [to throw], extends outward, hurling itself into the water to form a breakwater or outwork, a pier, or even the jutting of a natural promontory of rock. Smithson's sculpture, indubitably a spiral, curling inward rather than projecting outward, is the very opposite of the defining essence of a jetty. Moreover, the waters of Great Salt Lake have receded from the site that Smithson so carefully selected. The celebrated resurfacing of the work at the beginning of the twenty-first century was seen at first as a recalibration, a return to the natural balance of salt and rock and water that Smithson had envisioned. But in the decade since its reemergence, the waters have continued to retreat. As I write, they are over a half mile away. The lake, to be sure, is given to seasonal and periodic fluctuations, but exacerbated by climate change, and accelerated by the diversion of tributaries that have been détourned for farming and suburban development, they will not return to the site of the earthwork. Like the fern frond unfolding to gather sun, the *Jetty* might uncoil to strive, pining, for the waters in which it once bathed — reaching, aspirationally, with a strain at once pathetically desperate and longingly optimistic, toward the lake in which it once resided. With this new form, it would at last fulfill the last part of its name, and finally be a jetty proper.

In the final days of its slow unspooling, with a reverse recapitulation of its ontogeny, the *Jetty* would return to the shape

Smithson had originally conceived, before scrapping the form, demolishing the structure, and having the work entirely rebuilt, reluctantly, by the same crew who had just completed its construction, into an altered geometry. In place of the iconic, tightly coiled Pythagorean spiral of golden proportions with which we are familiar, Smithson had originally built a long pier curling at its tip, more whimsical than mysterious, like a question mark to its own existence, or some other mark of punctuation to interrupt the desert text in which it was inscribed, or, most of all: a fishhook to snare the legendary monster said to dwell beneath the bloody waters of the lake — waters which were otherwise far too salinated to sustain piscine life, its buoyant solution supporting only a single species of small shrimp and the larva of a fly.

The snake strikes; the clock strikes; a minor storm strikes land.

The Phaistos disc figures the spiral labyrinth as language itself, the minotaur of semantics waiting at the end of syntax with the double-edged axe of understanding.

After its surfacing from a watery seclusion, after three long decades of submerged occlusion, the silt recedes from the stones of the *Jetty* like gums pulling away from teeth — an abstringent gingival recession evincing in miniature the telluric logic that will soon maroon the purloined rubble in a desert plane so vast the boulders will appear like dust motes settled in an idle design by curling currents. Pilfered from the nearby hillside — with all the hybris of some demon choosing single atoms from the random movement of their Brownian bounce with a capricious cull, arranging them in order to figure a mercurial curve in willful imitation of Nature's occasional, unpredictable clinamenatic swerves but with an intention contrary to Nature's mindless, unmotivated error — the stones are stranded by an unanticipated dissipation of the sands, rescinding its initial situation, in a fugitive remove that even a sculptural imagination ruminating on the ruins of time never dreamed would come so soon.

The boulders are rounded and ground down along their ingrown jawline from gnawing at the winds.

Now evolving into a long reptilian epoch after a brief, amphibious phase in turn upon a lacustrine stage, emerging from its brittling chrysalis of salt crystals in a critical eclosion from a systole contraction of constringing coils to a diastolic, easing erosion, the purposeful formation appears, from a distance, like the grand, familiar form of Paleozoic cephalopods. But the connotation may be far more menacing: the fossilization of a nightmare after the cartilage of day has dissolved. In the waters that once rose above the now remote and desiccated rock-line of the *Jetty* swam *helicoprion*—a ponderous, chondrichthyan, carboniferous fish in sinister drift within the warm shallow Permian waters just off the southern shores of Gondwanaland. Like a shark from a fever-dream Boschian seascape it sported whorled dentition somehow once monstrously incorporated, inconceivably, into its anatomy, leaving fossils that look like ammonite with sharp incisors for the septa of their saddled sutures, its snarl set for chewing through the shallow prehistoric waters, or like the fearsome theomorphic ram's horn of the god of conquered Kush drowned by jealous Egyptian deities beneath an ancient inland sea, or else some giant nautilus with denticulated chambers in cuspidate arrangement—an ambuscade for any swimmer in the murky dusk of curling plumes of sediment disturbed by carangiformic oscillations, who crossing with the current would find themselves caught on the daunting, gaunt terminus of a curving keratin tusk.

The galeated crest of cormorous fangs commands a tremulous respect as its form tenses to a closed-fist curl: a centurion insignia salute of striking ordered might and monstrous cruelty of concentration.

The sinking masses nibble at the sands. Wind sibilates when mingling with the granular matrix, furrowing the grains in calibrated, wave-trough, serrate trenches.

The rough weave of the rain evaporates before it pocks the pumiced crust.

A sculpture castigates the grave, unbroken stretch of the terrain.

The great jaw masticates the space in which it clenches.

The snake coils; the clock winds; the storm clocks record winds.

In a widden-dream the symbol sketches out the logic of the ephialtes in a narrative trajectory of psychic conquest: skeletal elephants in battle-tassels over alps descend to sink beneath a *mare mortuum.*

Bacteria degrade the phenol at a rapid rate; acids batter at the peptides; the epidermis corrugates and bleaches; tepid waters balm the verrucated creases; bloating buoys floating bodies; tissue adipocerates.

Across the fissures of the mud cracks' crazed geometry the mandible intorts: unyielding, compact, logical, constricted as if by some immense gravitational grief. Wherever one may choose to look: mud, salt crystals, rocks; not a drop of water — every bit a dry, withered, threadbare, firm, hard field. The desert kiln of the bed convects. A twenty-Kelvin drop accompanies the night. The cooling crops and isolates impurities. The rate decreases to the dawn. Chondrigenous day swells back and then is once again abruptly gone. Such cycles perch the mineral lattice, which stretches, merging with the curve of earth, woven like a cloth which forms the ground on which embroidery is worked. Against this backdrop the crushing quirl of the rocks depicts the bitter champion of design, straining against every orthodoxy, quarreling with rectitude, while each vent marks a rent in the text of the image's decree, opening a mouth with which abstraction preaches: a maw, dentata, to devour even iconoclasm itself, and into which all experience rushes.

The snake charmer watches, with minor acridity, and then storms off.

A petulant petrel wheels from the shore.

The dream of the mythic San Buenaventura seemed unshakable. Over time, it became less a wishful hope for some navigable waterway, an easy conveyance for transcontinental commerce and migration, and more a necessity for maintaining the integrity of the natural world. The nineteenth-century imagination found it difficult to conceive that every stream did not aspire to sea. Into the Great Basin so desolate and vast the intrepid John Frémont was frightened even to enter it, trappers circled, certain that the laws of geometry together with those of riparian descent guaranteed they would intersect the Rio — christened with the holy waters of its own miraculous hopeful faith before it had ever been seen — at some point between the Rockies and the Sierra Nevada. They always returned, thirsty and perplexed. The mirage persisted, inverted: if it could not be found flowing over the desert surface, then it must be subterranean, draining from a tunnel beneath the great inland lake, with its remarkable salinization — a liquid desert more desert than the sands that surrounded it — corroborating its communication with the salty waters of the ocean. And if the lake sluiced out through some deep vent, then there must be a vortex of downward-rushing waters so fearsome it would splinter ships. Some of Frémont's party, including seasoned naval veterans, sent to circumnavigate the lake, were so sure of the inevitable maelstrom that they refused, out of fear, to leave the shore.

As late as 1870, boatmen from the anti-Mormon outpost of Corrine reported a great eddy off Fremont Island, threatening to draw in and capsize the schooner *Kate Conner,* captained by a colonel retired from a career of genocidal massacre and raids against Shoshone, which plied a route between the south-shore mines and the Montana Territory freight trails in the years before the Utah Northern Railway laid down narrow-gauge tracks for carriage to Cache Valley from a Union Pacific spur.

Petroglyph spirals abraded by Freemont peoples over fugitive pigment anthropomorphs grind time, forecasting future sympathetic drownings.

The military gabionage contains its fill with spacious cracks as if by magic and extends the causeway's course through pure force of will. Foam churned from the whisk of the wire mesh bleaches the beach.

From the gentle shallows soothing waters soon begin to move, quickening, in broad rotation—a depression appears, with a siren twist—then as swift as the sea nymph Thoösa, within her dark arching caverns, their vacant eye widens as they run, as if to stare into avernal depths so dry they fail to reflect the blinding sun above, exposing the sunken sediment on which abolished, waterlogged detritus, long settled, rests. The drowning grasp with all the folly of some Polyphemus feeling for the pearly wool of the Cyclops's flock.

The grinding stream winds to the core of the body's bed for solace and sorrows at its absence.

A pocket clock with purpose announces the moment of the hour with a certain curt finality.

The pilots on Great Salt Lake were not alone. A firsthand account, from the late eighth century, describes peering from the summit of a wave over the bare edge of a watery abyss known as the "navel of the sea": the unfathomable yawning of a depthless chaos; one of the secret currents of suck and vomit, fluid collapse and flotsam spew in which ships are swallowed, chewed, and retched as wrecks to wash in splintered timbers staved upon the shore. Windswept sand there corrugates from waves. Tattered canvas, with a feeble hold on torn and tangled rigging, flaps a surrogate panic, drowning horizontal in the gusts. The deluge pelts the foreshore with impressions that the drier sands absorb.

The inorganic world could, and does, exist in a kind of chaos, but before life can peep forth it has to have some kind of unofficial assurance of nature's stability, just as we have read that stability of forces in the ripples impressed in stone, or the rain marks on a long-vanished beach, or the unchanging laws of light in the orbed eye of a four-hundred-million-year-old trilobite.

The salt flats of the Great Basin west of Corrine are so level that the course of any eddy would reveal the Coriolis force impelling the direction of its spin.

The naiads' knowledge is seductive.

The kelpies tell the names of pain.

The rushing waters of the vortex speak to the shore with broken voices; their *stile brisé* arpeggiates the siren hiss that leaves the sailor vexed and torn: in terror at the irresistible attraction of the terrible last kiss of the spray from the gaping mouth of its inward curving lip.

With a look into Charybdis's abyss, the *Jetty* petrifies the siren's scream in a funerary monument to motion.

As Smithson understood, the whirlpool can be conquered, but only by placing it in proper perspective. As it grows, we must learn to cultivate that which must never be permitted to enter the maelstrom: the ineluctable logic of the non-laminar, which—if too complex to map or calculate—is nonetheless as determined, fated, and stable as the fall of a stone along the vertical vector, parsed independent of its arc, into the glassy smooth surface of a strangely buoyant lake.

The best sailors know that the most dangerous waters are not the roiling white of rapids and breakers but the placid, irenic appearance of deceptive, lulling calm.

The snake strikes; the clock strikes; the miners strake.

The gull swerves shoreward, her single wing's skin swept back by the wind, curving to a thin ellipse … lips kissing out in puffing pouts, billowing swells distending, then concaving in a sudden exhalation and impulsive retreat, with the pistoned pant of pneumatic bellows rounded out in punching bouts—the heaving beat of slung booms sung with canvas slaps and snapping sheets—as the prowling prow ploughs the turfed surface of tilled surf, a newly tilted cant briskly pitching to the bank, with high-skewed angles of yaw and little sign of damping, taking flight beneath the porous spume confused and calcinated white like fluid tufa; ranked rows advancing toward the scaw, across the sunken causeway, refraining in hydrographic canticles chanted like a choir of angels over yawning caverns in a chaos of cataclasmic chasms; reaching, zephyr impended, stressed pinions stretched before each sudden collapse, the surface soon smooths iron-flat, as if by the passing of some floating screed, then just as quick distressed, discrete—quills stalled in squalls of aqueous, scrawled calligraphs scripted by degrees like the ligatured arabesques of some furious caliph's impetuous, pent, tempestuous scrid decreed—flapped in fraught semaphores of repeated dilation and fleet diastolic release.

The boat, in short, floated upon the troubled waters.

Its iron hog-chain, taut, maintained (the structure, shallow-hulled, arched without a cinch to stay the sagging of the ark), despite the strain. Lacing traceries of salt brine wove over waves on which they rose and fell in gliding float, slickly slipping, assuming thin synaptic threads of froth before assimilating smaller nodes, and then distending, purging in dispersion—the process cycling over again in turn from ebbs attenuating in their drift to amalgamates subsuming; the surging spume in wroth, now rousing, spurged. Annealed by the unctuous slaver of the spindrift, the cambered hull, by nature punctual, was laved.

Following the mesoscale's sostenuto series of demotic *avisos furiosos,* in its isosmotic pressure, sailors sent lassos lashed as hawsers to provisos, the moorings anchored in desmostic, isosceles restraints, so soon cut through with Phrygian precision up to the ricassos by the wuthered flaying of sustained fletched laminae against untenable tensile detrusion — slack lashings frayed to glossoscopic symptoms as the ship's set sossling to the subsequent stillness of the silted, calm substratum of capsizal's newly ceilinged, quagged Sargasso Sea, which, were there some auditor, seems to be sospiring only with a basso's soss in full remorse, while no salvatic band of virtuosos — or even any lone, late sospitator, redeeming, arising — accedes.

The sailors' signals of extreme distress, morsed in morphing and repeated, urgent appeals, went, in brief, unheeded.

Brigham Young's pride and joy, the *Timely Gull* — the largest craft of any consequence to venture on the waters of the Great Salt Lake in the decade since the middle of the century, when Stansbury launched the *Salicornia,* itself a first-rate frigate, consorted by a skiff, trafficking with stately dignity upon the bosom of those solitary waters, circumnavigating, to make his mensual mensuration of its bleak and naked blood-red shores, without even a single tree to relieve the eye as he surveyed the lacustrine topography that framed the desolation's stillness of the grave below the distant peaks — had been of a sudden gale-ripped from its moorings at Black Rock and, in the heavy winter winds that rose in February's fury, tossed upon the petrose shore above the scuttling waves, in splinters, staved. Piled by the stormwinds' hostile pummel, the riven timbers would stay hidden by the self-same waters that had made its construction a necessity when they submerged the spit that had bridged a herd-path track to Antelope Island, until celebrating its sesquicentennial by raising up its beams above the brack again, in a palisade of paling stanchions driven in the sand. The deocculted pickets would appear to local shrimpers like the broken spears of some defiant phalanx sparring with the sky.

Snakes slough; axes prick.

Before Young fitted up his ship with grommeted garments of flaxen canvas waxed as sailing cloth, allowing the breath of god to speed it towards its purpose, two carthorses, martingaled like the dolphin-striker of *The Gull* herself, with tackle harnessed to a treadmill, in turn connected to a stern wheel, propelled the ship; the pair of equine trekkers walked upon the water, hyaline eyes fixed in the distance on the reflectance of a blinding luminescent destination — ever-receding and never attained. As they ambulate, clouds of midges, risen by the morning warmth, swarm and clamber; brine flies glaze the shoreline; the margin of the lake, in haze, conflates the horizon's halation with its minimal hypsographic measure. The horse-marines plod on across the halcyon waters of the salinated inland sea.

Young's cattle-barge had been designed and piloted by pioneer Dan Jones, a Welshman out of Halkyn, who had captained steamships on the Mississippi, navigating converts by the hundreds in pilgrimage upriver to Nauvoo. Freighted in its day with flagstone, cedarwood, and salt, *The Gull* was meant to carry livestock, ferrying Young's herds in seasonal rotation from periodic pastures on the long-grassed Lake isles and, against the impendent threat of Ute attack on shore, deliver them with swift elusion to the sanctuary of some saline keep, secure beyond defile, dangling at its scrap-iron anchor, long stay apeek, in tantalizing appropinquity, just out of earshot of the rancorous chorus of the battle cries and war whoops, even for the keen-eared quadrupeds. The skittish phobic bovine, though, would soon lapse back, amnesiac, settled in their placid taciturnity: impassively at ease, indifferent to the spectacle of distant hoof-stirred dust that shrouded raided ranching plats, immune in their abeyance, preoccupied only with the tranquil rustle of the breeze amid gramineæ.

Assuming that the average dairy cow extends to a length of around one hundred inches, and that they boarded arkwise, two by two, in double ranks upon the barge's tarred and mitred planks, and that the carlin of the *Gull* spanned a full forty-five feet, as widely reputed, it could have carried a score of cattle at a time in full continual transport. Supposing that the coil of *Spiral Jetty* were the scroll finial of a seventeenth-century viola da gamba, the strings of that mighty instrument would stretch to 2,176 feet, almost thirteen times the length of the intestine obtained from a prodigious specimen of a full-grown ox or steer, locally prized for the high collagen of its *submucosa* and *externa*. With the *peritoneum* soaked and *serosa* scraped and the surface steeped for days in a potash of potassium hydroxide, the tight-wound entrails can sound a dulcet timbre, almost vocal, when strung as strings, amber-hued and rosinous, attached from box to bridge. The lowest of those catgut cords would call for the sacrifice of roughly 184,320 animals, which would entail 9,216 voyages, accordingly, of the barge to deliver (and discounting the thousands calved in the interval so as not to leave the island vacant). Cruising at two horsepower, ship stowed to bale-cube capacity at twenty register tonnes, it would have taken Dan Jones a decade and three full months of steady sailing, in continuous loops from shore to shore without pause, to accomplish the conveyance. In order to maintain a baroque-era pitch, in even-temperament tuning, the D string of that gigantic jetty bass viol would require a tension of almost fourteen billion newtons. The force would thus be four thousand times the winds — deafening in themselves, coursing the shore and raking the sands — that once careened the great and mighty hull of the devastated *Timely Gull* in that fatal winter gale of 1858.

Locks pick; claims jump; wounds fang.

If one were to uncoil the modulated spiral groove from a standard 33⅓ LP record, letting the absorbent, inky carbon black warm in the desert sun, until the vinyl softened enough to begin to be pliable and plastic — not melting, quite, but malleable, with a viscosity of sound that could be straightened out under a careful, patient, constant tensile pressure to an acoustic smoothness — the hurried cursive script of the sound-writing, unkinked to a straight line, droning, drawn and followed from flux to true, a sonic exporrection from music to mere hum, in which any noise would be only the ring of the channel itself ravelling out, a paradox of static from motion, from the friction of the stylus through the groove, even without any collision with occasional grit — the mechanism registering itself registering — the stretch of that distended lathe-cut track would extend to exactly the length of the *Spiral Jetty*.

The mines are lined with brasque and graphite.

Gleaming with ridges like wave-fronts reflecting and masking, in parallel trenches of crest and crevice, the record would replace the play of water and rock that Smithson had envisaged as the essence of his project: mirror surfaces disconnected from each other, deconstructing any literal logic, dislocated into compass-point centers of gravity: a precarious balance in which gravity itself is lost in a web of possibilities, a centrifugal vortex pitting the vanishing point of the center against the solidity of the circumference in an agony of gravity within the force of the cyclonic, bending light rays with the massiveness of the planetary. The wandering and fixed change places. The mind seeks the axis, the pole of the telos, taxing attention as the pull of the gravity of perception increases at local anomalies, so that the mind is always being hurled outward towards the edge in intractable trajectories that lead to vertigo. The dizzying spiral yearns for the assurance of geometry. The jetty bends to an undifferentiated state of matter, in which sand replaces water, water seems to freeze as salt crystals, each forming a molecular lattice echoing the spiral of the jetty through its helix, encrusting the stones with an icy coat so convincing, even in the 110° heat and aridity, that one fears to slip—taking tentative steps, warily balanced, one's downward gaze pitching from side to side, picking out random depositions of crystals on the inner and outer edges while the entire mass echoes the irregular horizon with a vertiginous spin.

The rattlesnake coils; the miners strike; the clock ticks.

The unspun groove of a phonograph scaled to the length of the *Jetty* would, in turn, unturned, itself stretch to precisely the radius required for a rotating space station to achieve earth's gravitation at .1 revolution per minute, thus staying below the threshold of vestibular illusions and nausea due to cross-coupling acceleration when turning the head.

The same distance charts the depth of the low-velocity zone of the Moho in the Eifel field, which holds the same reach as the upward propagation of the semi-annual temperature oscillation in October and April at the Wollops Island, the "D" region of the ionosphere, the height of the mesosphere above the earth's surface, the thickest portion of the earth's crust, the average thickness of tectonic plates, the orbital distance of the Dactyl satellite from the asteroid Ida, the diameter of the large-impact structure associated with distal ejecta and the mass radiation of Acritarchs, which is also the diameter of the Chesapeake impact structure, with its tektite-strewn field, equal to the predicted deflection of the summed sinistral displacement of the slip on the Mammoth Wash, or the length of the continuous reef that fringes the Tanimbar Islands, just north of Yamdena, a span at which bowheads overflown by a Twin Otter dive.

In 1910, aviator Alfred Leblanc covered the distance in one hour and eleven minutes and fifteen seconds, though it took over twenty-five minutes longer with the addition of a passenger (Léon Morane, however, was able to complete the course in just under an hour, clocking in at the finish-line at fifty-nine minutes and fifty-two seconds, even with two passengers on board), while in 1947 William Odom flew his Teterboro modified A-26 Invader around the entire world in the same time. The age of the air race had of course been preceded by the rush of the locomotive: the lust for the steam-driven celerity of steel wheels not merely spinning but skating on rails faster than their friction could grip; in 1891 the special passenger train of Jason "Jay" Gould, ruthless robber baron of the gilded age, whose own private car was christened not *The Argos* but *The Atalanta,* after the goddess of speed (perhaps forgetting, or perhaps insisting, that she had been derailed in her race by the lure of golden apples), traveling from Council Bluffs to Chicago, could have traversed the straightened length of the *Jetty*-sized groove in an hour. Even in 1913, the *D-Züge* Reichsbahn express could do no better, keeping pace with the fast-approaching automobile, though even the twenty-seven-horsepower Pathfinder, at the time exhibiting the best performance of an American car on the banked circuit at Brooklands, adjacent to the aerodrome, could only tie the locomotives, at the very moment Marcel Duchamp, strolling through the Salon de la Exposition de la Locomotion Aérienne with Fernand Léger and Constantin Brâncuși, was drawn up short before the aerodynamic torque of a propeller, a helical prop at once biomorphic in its curves and cruelly mechanical, remarking, "painting is dead; who today could do anything better than this propeller?" Years earlier, the seductive sleek of industrial design inspired Filippo Tommaso Marinetti to proclaim "a roaring automobile, which seems to run on the grapeshot path of cannonfire, is more beautiful than the *Victory of Samothrace.*" Nike of the race, proudly acephalic, strides on the waves, wings bent backward with the curve of an aerofoil. It was the same year Franz Kafka, together with Max Brod and his brother, fresh from their Italian holiday, would pulse through the crowd, with Futurist hurry and haste, overtaking the leisurely, threatening to leap over food carts, impatient to arrive at the dusty artificial wasteland built for the airshow at Brescia — a desert of prescient dreams. Most of the planes never left the ground.

At whatever speed, the distance of the distended groove would be equal to the total length of the Estrada de Ferro São Eduardo ao Cachoeira do Itapemirim, or the route from El Prado to Cascade on the San Joaquin and Eastern line through California, traveling the Southern Pacific and switching to the Big Creek, or the run of the Hornos line to the ninth marker in Mexico, or the total of all the lines of the Marquette and Southeastern Rail Road, which equal the average mileage run per drive per day of eight hours steaming in Western Australia in 1927, which matched the tracks proposed to be laid from Typiza to Quiaca, on the Argentine frontier, or later, at a cost of 250,000 Pounds Sterling [$15,304,420 dollars today] from Yanacancha to Chilete, in Peru, which represents the range of the Toyota iQ microcar on a full battery, which would have let it cruise all of the existing roads in the Upper Charley subwatershed at the turn of the 21st century, which is just the length of the belt of lignite deposited during the Tertiary period in the geological age known as the Oligocene-Miocene in the productive zone of the Chilean provinces of Concepción and Arauco, the distance to the west/southwest of Ma'sal of Haliban at the time of Himyar control, to the east of the Shatt to the port of Bandar Shapur, the widest point of the Qatar Peninsula, the length of the Golan Heights, the width of Lebanon, smallest country in the Levant, Babylon south from Baghdad, Yongbyon, Los Alamos of Korea, north from Pyongyang, Lake Naivasha, floricultural exporter, northwest from Nairobi, Jinja, on the shore of Lake Victoria, near the source of the White Nile, northeast from Kampala, the Kingdom of Ayutthaya north of Bangkok, Cambridge northeast from London, Chartres south from Paris, Alençon from Lisieux.

Fangs maim; springs unwind; abandoned claims are mined.

The polyvinyl groove of bromides and cyclanes, once unspooled, would cover the stretch of the Haida Gwaii marine, the run of the Western Ghats inland from the Arabian Sea, pocked with crumbling rock-cut Buddhist caves and honeycombed with apsial halls and humble cells that served as meditative havens, like the shrine of El Brezo, the same unspun distance northwest past Obeso on the border of the Cantabrians with the Castillan plains, founded by pilgrims from Extremadura who travelled over two hundred years to find the site perched on the cirque at the foot of a faraway peak, as distant as the known measure of the Campine Basin, from northwest to southeast, stretching its coal seam from Limburg to Antwerp, the strike of the Idaho rift system of fissures, vents, spatter cones, feeder dikes, ramparts, frozen surges, back-drained coatings and blown ash, or the San Bernardino Mountains from Cajon Pass to San Gorgonio Pass, the same distance from Emerald east to the Jellinbah open-pit mine or Leonora northeast to the Thunderbox gold mine and north to the underground Waterloo nickel mine or Attawapiskat west to the Victor open pit or from Buchans South to the Duck Pond Mine or Niamey West to the Samira Hill Mine or Tha Luang northeast of Phuket or Tambol Tabkwang northeast of Bangkok or Kaeng Khoi to the north or Dorows west of Mutare which is the trip distance on the Ruta Nacional 40 west to Parque Nacional Perito Moreno on Ruta Provincial 37 as far as Moalboal southwest from Cebu City or Tucson southwest to the observing facilities on Kitt Peak or Kyushu to the mountainous summits and sub-sea-level valleys of the island of Tushima, feared pirate base during the thalassocracy of antiquity—as terrifying and as far as the stretch of ocean, out of sight of land, explored in an open canoe by Pleistocene sailors from Sahul to the Manus Island, now the length of the magical, comforting, deep-forest runs of cross-country ski trails outside Oslo specially lighted for exclusive evening tours, which is as far away as Dr. Awótáyọ̀'s hospital from the noted herbalist Dr. Akinolá, or the extent of faulting, with spectacular surface ruptures along the Stillwater Range, or the span of the Baetis navigable by ancient Roman merchants, keen to barter from their large ships, past hateful rebel Sertorians to Hispalis, which traveled the length of the slough south of the Burmese Palace of Mandalay to the Kinda Irrigation Scheme strengthening the run-of-the-river schemes built a thousand years earlier, a flow equaling the sewer system in Lima, Peru, at the time of the First World War, or the maze of cast-iron mains of the water-supply system of Shamokin at the same moment — all as distant as the gap between continents, where Asia and North America warily approach one another, at the Bering Strait.

The raxed wax unribbons, portending. Following the vertiginous logic of the spiral, one continues, imperceptibly, to reverse course without even noticing; continuing in one direction leads to the opposite. Another paradox: the considerable work required to uncoil the carefully etched spiral accelerates the façade of an entropic state — everything at undifferentiated rest and extending to the horizon in a uniform, heat-death stillness — that belies the effort needed to simulate it.

The recording, analogue, compacts without compression.

The crests of the frozen, alkali wave-fronts recode the motion of the shore of the shott. They take the form of the foam as a sandstone paragon. The mainland oscillates; the lake remains rock-still.

The lock groove, compassing the spindle, clicks.

The gastropod retracts. The beveled crystal case refracts. The hour chimes.

The sabkha crops as the saline surfaces.

The kavir covers with a friable crust.

Brack recedes; brine steeps; the shore pulls back.

The flats crack with fractal patterns.

The revolutions keep the time.

Surface noise startles the listener—a plosive breaks the lull of the hiss and the comfortable hum is drowned by a crackle, distracting.

The snake tricks; the gears trip; miners strip.

The shellac, sounding its lack, with the track of the wavering, compacted vermiculate groove like the path left by a distracted bark beetle boring through its dark arboreal palace of galleries frassed in a labyrinth of audible tracery and tremulous phonography—half determined perseverance and half ennui, attempting to replicate the annual annular pattern of its host, recapitulating its dark marks of dendrochronology in reverse, through the lignin toward the pith—in an agitated calligraphy of tibial ambulation, a dance of digestion leaving the choreography of blind hunger, waiting to be read by whatever sympathetic mechanism could decipher and sound it, brittles and threatens to snap at the least, careless impact.

The case unlocks. The seeds scatter over soil. The groove serrates like crémaillères.

Coil, spring, strike.

The medium is a matter of scale. A varnish of shells, from Kerriidae, *une laque en écailles,* once dyed the substrate of their melted plates with a red like the lake staked by Smithson in the midst of a bloom of halophilic archaea, shading themselves from the desert sun's ultraviolet radiation with clouds of carotenoids.

The color vanishes under carbon. The resin sheens.

The shore of the lake becomes the edge of the sun. Categories dissolve.

Surrounded by a chaos of cracks, an infinity of surfaces spreads in every direction.

The desert, as far as the eye can see, flattens — then shimmers at the horizon like a vast sea rippling at the shore of the sky. The beach of the heavens rises from sight.

Perched on rampikes of stone, petrified birds sing petrified songs in the stillness of petrified forests — a fossilized silence of melody frozen in sweetness — their crystal quartz has been tuned to receive waves from radio towers of silicate trunks. Stands of timber, once wild and sylvan, measure the octaves in chiseled gradations. Plumes plummet from a gust, swirling in a vortex, with a measured avoirdupois; the sands impound. Saxifical arias in fading cadences along vertical axes resolve, necrophonic, with a *port de voix.*

Salt impedes freezing but propagates waves with accelerant speed.

The stylus retraces with a perfect devotion; it wavers, unwavering.

Pin is to pining as needle to need.

The priests lacked Latin but proceeded to preach. Silvestre Velez de Escalante, in search of the Buenaventura west to the Missions, was told of the great bitter sea he had neared, and turned back, returning to Santa Fe rather than face it. He christened it, unseen, as *Laguna de los Timpanogos* — ostensibly the lake of the Timpanogot tribe: those, like the rivers feeding the lake, from the rock [*tumpi*] and canyons [*panogos*]. But the Spanish missionary would have heard *timpano* ringing behind the word: the tympanum, or eardrum veiling the cochlea.

Skin, in the desert, leathering, tautens.

The caul tenters, blocking the mouth of the labyrinth.

The lake leaches asphalt to alkali, a thick viscous tar-seep escaping the faulting at Rozel Point, where halophiles metabolize the film of petroleum coating the shore. Salt and oil: the basic ingredients of a vinyl record.

If a phonograph were scaled to the size of the *Jetty,* it would take fifteen kilograms of chlorine (salt) and eleven kilograms of ethylene (oil) to press the disc, the grooves of which would be as wide as the first glume—nerved, scaberulous, acuminate, with scarious margins—of the immaculate japonicus Thunberg Brome, once gathered for crithomancy and strewn upon carcasses, or the width of the hooded, glabrous, slender, distending stem—pale, buff-brown with a purplish tinge—of the rarely seen wood herb of the *Moringa* that skirts shaded glens, or of the coriaceous and strongly involute lemmas, *Perigyniae*—some ringed, some broadly ovate and others suborbicular, some flat, with the capsule, obvoid, retuse apically, much longer than the perianth, the achenes, and even some of the fruits and pods, to adumbrate the flora of Alberta, in the run of the Rockies north of the Wasatch—or the olive-pale, fimbriate or sometimes shortly dentate petals and long, spreading sepals of varieties of *Verticordia,* or the curt, asymmetrical, vertical calyx of Peruvian *Solanum salasianum,* alternately going out into the high mountain sun, and soothing in the shaded night of curtained rooms, or the narrowly ovate spathes of *hydrilloides* and the narrowly lanceolate lamina of spidering *silvicola,* the spikelets and awns of the lowest lemma of octoflora in the dry sandy spaces of roadsides in Kentucky, the loosely clustered sporocarps, borne midway along the stipes and shallowly saddle-shaped, or slightly biscoctiform, of various heterosporous semi-aquatic ferns curling from spirals and silently rising to the surface of shallow seeps to float their flowers in skeins that pattern ponds like the foil-gilt screens of a Japanese wind-wall—all the size of the scarce purple and gold *chrysolepidellae*: *Monochroa tenebrella* flying in the sun; the tarn-edging sweet-reed-seeding and Brome-boring *Elachista,* with *parametriotidae* and *momphidae* mining the leaves of enchanter's nightshade and great willowherbs, or resting in rough, damp areas, hibernating, cooling on willows with their white-tipped antennae; or the entire strongly granulose, ferruginous, and fuscous body of the tobacco cutworm in its second instar, captor to *polistes*—from parasol paper nests—or the stiff strand of the ovipositor of an *anastrepha* fruit fly, with incipient pectoral rays. None of which could thrive on the shores of Great Salt Lake.

Having left behind the realm of precision engineering and instruments machine-tooled to a microscopic caliber, measurable only with calipers of light, the sonic inscription of the expanded phonograph has risen to a botanical scale, and to the anatomy of insects in scamper among the grasses that shade them.

Snake, time, wage.

The groove width, a winding slot-canyon too shallow still to offer shade from the high desert sun, would measure the change in the effective evapotranspiration in the loess belt in March.

Equal to the height of the bands used to track common bird species of the sub-Antarctic forests of the Magallanes, or the diameter of the nylon lines in a omnidirectional passive barrier trap suitable for collecting those ravenous, lignigraphic bark beetles, or the required width of the white stripe in the "flammable solid" symbol placard scripted in Franklin Gothic Condensed and placed square-on-point before being affixed to portable cargo tanks transported by truck or rail, the grooves would just hold the smaller size of granular rubber shreds seeded in concrete mortar to control seasonal expansion, or accommodate the vertable screw rods inserted into the cortical shell-cancellous core, which is precisely the diameter of the medullary canal, at a point some 65mm from the tip of the olecranon, past which it becomes difficult to insert a screw, or the size of the ulnar drill hole made just at the tubercule of the supinator crest, the same size as the standard tip, per regulation, of approved periodontal probes of either style, the point below which end-diastolic wall thicknesses are likely to represent transmural scars and will not recover function, having lost their contractile reserve, which is also the smallest category of preoperative pupil size evaluated, equal to the point at which the medial rectus attaches to the sclera, and the point above the base of the perianth tube where the corona is fused, which is the distance of the ampulla to the posterior semicircular canals on the posterior face of the petrous of the internal acoustic meatus that would listen to the disc.

That listener could hear, on just one side of a *Jetty*-sized LP, all of Richard Wagner's Bayreuth-worthy operas (excepting, that is, *Die Feen, Das Liebesverbot,* and *Rienzi*)—fully *twice over,* so that one wouldn't have to choose between the stereo versions conducted by Solti and Karajan, while the B side could accommodate the complete symphonies of Mozart, Haydn, Beethoven, Bruckner, Mahler, Tchaikovsky and Shostakovich combined (sorry Brahms; sorry Sibelius), or the *oeuvre,* almost entirely unrealized, of Kaikhosru Shapurji Sorabji, or the entire current Morton Feldman discography, or Karlheinz Stockhausen's *Licht,* with a three-and-one-half hour intermission between each opera, for dining and relieving and brief naps before the next of *Die Tage der Woche,* all spun, *Fortstimmung,* from nineteen bars of a musical kernel, and with four helicopters [from the Greek ἕλιξ (spiral) + πτερόν (wing)], in the third scene of the *Mittwoch,* or four complete performances of Erik Satie's *Vexations,* or a very brisk, abbreviated rendition of the opening tacet of John Cage's *ASLSP.*

In the time it takes to play Side A, one could watch the entire run of ABC's *The Middle,* with CBS's *Numb3rs* binged while Side B plays, or NBC's *That Show with Joan Rivers* streaming for the duration of one side and *The Garfield Show* exhausted by the other, or the Colombian telenovela *Pasión de Gavilanes,* all the way to the happy ending, but not before the fight, mired in quicksand and mud, between Fernando and Dínora, who is bitten by a poisonous snake and dies, delirious, absorbed by the primeval jungle into which she had fled, paired with B.R. Chopra's record-setting, viewer-favorite *Mahabharata,* including Ayub Khan as Parikshit, killed by a venomous naga, cursed by Kadru, who nonetheless escapes the slaughter of the *yajña* of the Sarpa Satra and its unholy holocaust of serpents.

By the time both sides were played, the lecture and practical-work requirements in general zoology for first-year students in a natural science degree would be met, introducing them to the basic structures and processes by which the grooves of the disc could be measured in botanical and entomological terms, or, for an alternative career, the same time could be devoted toward the average pharmacology instruction of physicians' assistants at the turn of the millennium, or the requirements for Chinese flight attendants in courses on makeup, aviation history, and the psychological effect of colors on passengers. Time being money, such courses would be investments in future paychecks and advancements, and the same period would serve as the minimum amount of overtime required to be performed by an investigator for the Alcohol and Tobacco Tax division to be eligible for 15% premium pay, which was the median number of teacher absences in the 1986–87 school year, and the increase in wage hours over the decade between 1979 and 1989 by the average worker, while in the same shift Belle E. Powers and Mrs. L.B. Carlisle were paid $39.25, Laura Ensign, Eva Fleming, Mirian Woolon Brooks, Grace Troutner, Mrs. John J. Ruvane, Maisy Schreiner, and A.W. Moore were paid $39, and Alice Altoona was paid $23.40, as readers for the State Board of Education Exam in Iowa at the end of the first decade of the 20th century, which was more than enough time for John Self, Joe Shumake, and L.C. Watson to work the grounds (at 30 cents an hour), Sam Cook, Elgin Wadelich and A.W. Wilhite (at 85 and 5/7 cents an hour) with A.J.P. Barnes and W.W. Coulter (at 71 and 3/7 cents an hour) to work admissions, while Alice Hockins (at 25 cents an hour) with Geo. Chitsu and Jim White (at 30 cents an hour) worked the toilets, while Tom Sanders worked as lineman (earning 85 cents an hour) for the State of Missouri in 1921, or to complete the regular assignment of Stewards on trains Numbers 5 and 6 operating between Houston and Los Angeles via Lake Charles during the month of September, 1939 (earning $61.23), the working hours, in the third week of five days for the month of December, 1891, clocked by passenger-engine drivers on the 7:45am Dunfermline and Glasgow passenger train, which was the entire length of the rail journey from Simla to Madras, the dead-freight days per car on the East St. Louis Junction, the average detention of freight cars in Altoona, in March, 1917, requiring reconsignment, and taking the car and all those with which it is associated out of the current of traffic, the time cars in an eastern city were worked, while held on the tracks with stores including apples, oranges, bananas, lemons, cabbage, celery, cauliflower, and grapes, which was the time needed to bind harvests by hand in Campiña in the 1880s, or the work week under the two-platoon system of firefighting, paying due regard to the public interest, in Sydney and Newcastle, or the average time worked in collieries around Nottingham one June in the late nineteenth century, the decrease in time worked in the lath industry in Wisconsin the same year, the average contribution, per person per year, working ten-hour days, for the monumental building projects of a toutorix, or the days lost per employee previous to the erection of an institutional hospital, the increase in an individual's lifetime number of chronic-illness days for each additional unit of total suspended particulate matter in their atmosphere, the time, burning, it takes a frosted incandescent lamp to descend to eighty percent of its initial mean horizontal candlepower.

The same period could also be monetized as the twenty-thousand-dollar difference between the operation surcharges applied for postponements at Cape Vincent (downbound) or Cape Saint-Michel (upbound) on Lake Ontario, which is the advance notice required by non-national fishing vessels prior to entering Croatian ports, or the period of the float of corks in salt water before being wiped very dry on their surfaces, but not squeezed, before being weighed off the Isle of Wight, which is how long it takes to ride along a level road, keeping generally an east-south-east course, from the Hex river to the Swarte Berg which commences at the Touws Mountains and therefore must be considered part of the so-called Straat, the reduction in travel time for the express postal route from Berlin to Munich by way of Cologne by the end of the 1840s, which were the total flying hours clocked at Marshall's School in Cambridge, for the week ending 19 September (1937), including Mr. Gallyon's solo flight and the completion of Mr. Turner's tests, an underwater endurance record set by John Gary (almost doubling his own earlier record), the reduction in language service weekly direct broadcast hours by Voice of America between 1987 and 1992, the hours per week of broadcasts beamed to Africa by Radio Berlin International in 1975, the current-affairs programming broadcast each year by ITV, the hours devoted per week to national-service-type programs by the Trans-Canada network in 1965.

Those time slots measure survival times for the pigeon, when a smaller member of its species, in response to hypothermia, or the time for European Starlings to reach 50% mortality on a 100mg/kg chlordane diet or the point at which falconoid herpes virus infection becomes chronic or the median lethal feeding period, with 95% fiducial limits, for medium-sized rice-field rats, with grizzled yellow-brown and black pelage that is not spiny when stroked, in Parit Buntar, or the minimum time taken each month to sort and produce a mensural summary report using multipart handwritten forms in the Orange County Vector Control District (regarding mosquitoes, midges, flies, rats, and fish) which is the time it takes irradiated mice to die after being tested with the new Cysteamine derivative compound (#1109) which is the average survival of tame grouse released into the wild, the average time spent by hunters in the regular West River (South Dakota) herd-harvest season, the low-activity participation for visiting zoos in Mississippi, the average duration of larval instar for olive leaf-moths during the winter, the longer life span of second-generation Codling Moths, the average preoviposition period of all female corn borers and the maximum pre-pupal stage of bolls, a period which sees the mean duration of shedding Herpes in non-transplanted lagomorph eyes and the average duration of the fever exhibited by rhesus monkeys with yellow fever after intercerebral viral inoculation as well as the average duration of the third febrile attack in the apyretic intervals of relapsing fever from bilious typhoid and the average pre-admission illness period for charity patients with acute pediatric appendicitis which was the time between successive occupants of pernoctated ward beds, on average, per month, at St. Bartholomew's in 1871, the cyclicity of cytomegalovirus infection in infants, and the average lessening of the period of menstrual flow in after life.

The same duration spells the inflammatory suppression possible with the administration of 6mg betamethasone and the average time to cure bronchopneumonia with broncopulmonary complications treated by antibiotics as well as the plasma half-life of patients not previously hypersensitive to *L-asparaginase,* which marked the febricula treatment period for zymotic and constitutional diseases in the late nineteenth century, the net doubling time for exponentially increasing *Synechococcus* abundance on account of a spring storm in 1981, the maximum variance of cloudage between March and May over tropical Africa in 1975, the interval between the last observation at Arica, which was made with the sextant, and the first observation at Arequipa, which was made with the transit, the minimum transit time on shipments from Atlanta to Birmingham in the winter of 1959 which was precisely the time it takes volatile matter to decompose to twenty per cent of its original in sewage or the steeping time, in guano, of oats and *sandy oats* by Mr. McLintock, farmer from Locknick, near Pollock, who had always been troubled with smut and the reaction time of buffered digesters on account of calcium carbonate precipitate or the period over which the oral ingestion of urea by normal subjects correlates with a decreased rate of glucose disappearance from the blood equal to the critical value of solid-retention time for maximizing the gas production and gas yield rate in the anerobic digestion of swine wastewater in the tropics which is the time it takes a wave to propagate to the Farfield from the Ridge or the period with which tides enter from San Pablo with low silica concentration as a tidal stream flows back up the Sacramento and San Joaquin Rivers or the shipping time from Croatia to Antwerp or for light steam boats to make the run from Toulouse to Béziers in 1825 before the seventy-eight locks of the canal had to be navigated or the period between new trades in equity index futures according to stress-indicator tests in 2010 and the statistical number of Opposition days granted to the New Democratic Party in the first semester of the Supply period and the average stay of German tourists in Rome, which is the time lag between admission and reception of radiological and laboratory investigation reports in an Indian gynaecological hospital, the effective half-life of Iodine-131 in the environment under the conditions existing in Humboldt County, the half-life of gallium, the time it takes to read the Bible straight through, without pausing to eat or sleep or stretch or rest — a surplus at the end of every Chang cycle, leaving a lunar and solar misalignment, not cancelled until the nineteen-year period has been repeated eighty-one times, returning the universe to its original state every 1,539 years.

Then again, the *Jetty* itself might be played like a phonograph, to try and hear the music of geology, to amplify the sound written by the lithic inscription of erosion and displacement — a stone with the sound of its own making. With a boxcar cartridge and beam-crane tonearm, a needle could be run between the jagged inside line of the boulders, playing the phonolithic groove, registering the sinusoidal line of the rocky perimeter. Whatever music might emerge, it would be stupefyingly loud and deep — an infrasound not heard so much as felt, in a brute, dominating physicality, the hearer at once stunned by the amplitude of the volume, and then the feeling as if the listener were underwater, or rather something thicker than water, lungs fighting to push against the waves pressing them back with a respiratory rhythm all its own, and at frequencies as low as 7Hz beginning to pulse in sympathetic vibration with the brain's theta rhythms, provoking visceral, limbic terror and rage, then nausea as the internal organs pulsate with a new tidal tempest at work in the liquids of the body, ablaze with internal frictions never before felt, beginning to pulp as the organism strains, panicked, paroxysmal, to hear beyond the silence of its newly deafened state, though even if the ears still functioned, the source of the torment would be neither auditory nor locatable, seeming at first to come from everywhere, before the sickening sense that it was in fact coming from within the churning surf of the ocean of the liquefying body that had sought it.

The Cold Spring strike renegotiates the scales.

The purgatorial door of perception turns on the pin of a hinge of adamantine, resonant metal, like the stone around the spindle of a lithophonic *Jetty*, thunderous as the sub-sub-octave of a sixty-four-foot organ stop, drowning out the choir praying in soprano supplication to the greatness of the revelation symbolized by the negation of their statement in a deafening diapason.

Victims of such sound might dimly realize, behind the nebulous disorienting churning, as their heads felt as though they might split, that the coronal suture of the skull itself bears a certain similarity to the closely wavy line which the needle of a phonograph engraves on the receiving, rotating cylinder of the apparatus, as if some originary, fetal cry were captured in a prenatal cranial recording of its founding statement, the unheard announcement of a first urge to speak, emblazoned on the brain case that would contain the consciousness able to someday recognize the nature of the script and perhaps develop the technology to play it back—the interior essence inscribed on the outer surface of a first cry finally heard with a lifespan's belatedness. And then to expand outward, wondering what variety of lines, occurring anywhere, could not be put under the needle and sounded? Is there any contour that could not, in a sense, complete in this way and then experience it, as it makes itself felt, thus transformed, from the visual to the sculptural to the audible? The phonographic grooves of nature are thus read as the signatures of Creation which in the skeletal, mineral, and myriad places persist in remarkable, unique, versions and variations on a theme: the grain in wood, the gait of an insect, the faulting of the earth, the fracture of ceramics .... every line that attracts the eye with its zig-zag pattern newly open as an auditory event when the visual sounds with styli that read instead of write.

The watch chimes; the miners strike; the snake rattles.

After the needle drops on the *Jetty*-sized phonograph, as the first notes are played, the angular momentum (assuming at 33⅓rpm) clocks at almost 105 meters-per-second, with a radial acceleration of 365 meters-per-second-squared, exerting a force of 1,187.56 newtons on the ring of basalt rocks — well over the point at which window glass will be shattered by the sonic booms of test jets from the Dugway Proving Grounds, the tension forces transmitted through the riser line of the parachute payload system released from that jet, with the bridle at full length, six seconds after deployment, the thrust of each operating engine of the booster stage of the Saturn 1 rocket, the load deflection on the strut spring of one of the tripod legs of the landing gear of a lunar vehicle on a nonlevel surface with honeycomb aluminum shock absorbers, the tensile strength of hot-rolled and heat-tempered nickel–copper alloy bars, the requirements for a typical, conservatively designed ram, the pull of the mass of the earth on a typical human body, standing at its surface, the intradiscal pressure associated with shear loading and bending of the spine, when standing, with load torsion and compression creating torque forces, the axial force on bone plugs lacking helical threads, the static pressure at which intact monkey spinal columns failed, fifteen times the force required to fracture the human skull — in short: over one megajoule on a bejeweled, diamond-dust stylus.

Like the spindle at the center of the turntable—its name, even with the intrusive d of later forms, like a spill from which a line unspools, perhaps like a splinter of bone, a slip or a sliver of twisted scrap iron, a filament of ingot, or paper twisted to light a taper, related not to *spine* but to spinning, like the Swedish *spinnil* [spider], the name also given, because of their appearance in the record of the hypnogogic borders of sleep to the amplitude of the waves that build regularly to a maximum and then fall regularly again, a barcarole of consciousness lulling itself to dream, creating a configuration seen in an electroencephalogram—the spine also seems to aspire to stand firmly upright.

The column is a compass needle that in pointing toward the solar star to which it stretches inevitably also indexes downward toward the gravitational center of the earth as well, under the psychogeophysical forces that conspire against us and that open the chthonic to the imagination, entangling the subterranean with a sense of self—the proper and the propertied confused by the course of an evolutionary morphology. The orientation causes us to question the very coordinates of identity and to wonder about the unseen beneath our feet: what happens if a hole were dug straight down? What would be found there?

The implications for genre follow, as an art form goes hand in hand with the birth of the science of geology: landscape is not merely a frontal view, a panoramic sweep across a horizon concealing the vanishing points of binocular perspective, but landscape is also something behind or above your head as well as underneath your feet. You are not only the compass and measure, an axis that defines but does not enter the field of vision—now you are an integral part of the landscape, an extension of place, a subject of the magnetic gaze of a gravitational stare that looks through you as you try to establish the field that is more mirror than demesne.

The prolonged spinal trajectory summons a sense of the earth's three-dimensional properties: land as not merely as a horizonless lateral extension but a telluric mirror that drills imaginatively down to counterbalance the upright thrust from the walking hominid who reaches toward the sky, with all the gesture's Romantic aspirations, to be sure, courting the sublime of the galaxies and most distant stars, but now counterbalanced by the enslaving covetousness of hypogenic property—the mine of possession.

A prolonged spinal trajectory accounts not only for our locomotion, but also for our litigious curiosity: a long-standing enlightenment concern with exactly how far property rights extend downward into the earth's mantle.

The yield of the new genre of landscape is similarly abysmal: extractive mining, terrestrial drilling, lesioning terraformation .... every wound of the surface of the earth results from our orthostasis. The twisted labyrinthine path following from every footprint, again and again, turns out to be the vertical axis of the body's bony ledger, a mnemonic chronicle in a three-dimensional script of precise and undecipherable language: the cord with its vertebrae knotted like khipu, asserting and ascertaining, registering with a granular accounting, an ossified text—parallel to the textile record of Incan domination along an Andean ridgeline—in its compendium of unspeakable crimes.

Body whose bones are no longer and already lithic, heart more and already wave, belly more and always beach.

Every pencil drawing from the 14th century on can be seen as a nonsite sculpture, remapping the graphite mines of Seathwaite, Cumbria or Huehna in southern Spain.

The spring snakes; the watch chimes; the manners mind.

The greensward, verging from the bed above the surf, clumps in tufts as if from denshiring or burnbaiting and cuts to a dendrical feather-edge, shading the bends of the sward of turf from the bluff. A sparrow makes its brief flight through the warmth and light.

The Ancients believed that snakes were born from the marrow of the spine.

The form divines an anticipatory past with its ophidiomantic prediction of the future of our petrifying fate. Self-absorption reified and raised to the level of mathematical precision, the curl of the *Jetty* turns its back on the imperative of the species's specious narrative, refusing to conclude with the arrow-straight backbone that would seem to be the climax of our evolutionary telos. Developing against gravity, hominids fell upward over the millennia, straining to straighten in a perpendicularization: a bodily geometry that will come to privilege the rational gridded rectitude of the orthogonal as the brain projects the anatomy of its support outward to the mathematical, philosophical, and ethical.

Shading the eyes from the afternoon sun risks a *pavor diurnus*, a fever-dream realization that consciousness might not resurface, unable to face the light.

With every upright step and counterbalancing swing of the arms, lording over the earth with a forward stride, we commemorate the Late Ordovician fight against gravity and the logic of verticality that the era pursued: certain plants began to develop stiff vascular stems, a central chordate appeared in certain animals. As the trees soared upward on their trunks, evolution worked to slowly uncurl the chordate. With spiral columns unafraid of time, the path constructs a labyrinth that awaits an evolutionary Theseus, caught in a physiological trap and faced with the problem of escaping his own ingenuity. Cephalization, however, provides the Ariadne's thread of time, unspooling a cord from the ravelled mass of its knotted ball.

What then is the spinal column, if not a megalith raised to the mineralizing trace of the organism's diaspora into its own expanding sensorium: the interior skeleton an outward memory of inward collapse. The chthonic externalizes its mineral core, disseminating and propagating through the calcifying skeletal tether of the brains that in their orthospinal loft will come to contemplate the depths from which they titrated and petrified, externalizing their organs in lithic turn. Ever higher, the chamaeprosopic skull adorns the monument of time — a cranial cairn on a radial pillar, a metronome marking the pace of survival, a terrestrial crinoid uprooted and moving.

Ever deeper, the mine sculpts a cenotaph to man-made systems mired in abandoned hopes.

Scholiasts note the discrepancies.

Circumscribing an insistent horizontality, and diametrically opposing the imperative to extend straight into the water, as anything *jetée* should do, the *Jetty* appears like the final scoliosis of what were once called "formed stones" — the point at which *spinal* and *spiral* converge as conceptual and not merely verbal approximations, as in the German *Wirbel,* the word denoting both vertebra and vortex. Each osseous whorl is a cyclone in time. The whole stands as a talisman against the carnage of a spinal catastrophism; telluritropic, it forges a fetish against all of the psychic ailments, neuroses, and hallucinated nightmares that are ultimately afflictions of the spine in its orthogradic pathology.

At the same time, apotropaic, the spiral anticipates the viral, warding off the helical capsids of coronavirus, their rotational matrices encoded with folded axial symmetry, so that the RNA spirals out, multiplying through the organism from mucus membranes to the thalamus to the laminae, in a retrograde direction, incubating in the buoyant, warm lymphatic bath of cerebrospinal fluid.

The snake strikes; the clock strikes; the miners strike.

Winding through an osseous maze the membranous labyrinth faces the internal acoustic meatus and contains myriad fenestrations, the stapes calling from the incus through an oval window as the whole thrums around the modiolus, projecting bony shelves of divided spiral lamina, a staircase wending down toward the organ of Corti.

The ring of the anvil granulates from piercing urgency to shimmer.

The ring of the horizon shimmers at an angle as the baked pan's gravel purges radiation.

The Northern shrike, in annual cycles, returns from tundra and winters in the shrub. Its strong beak's angled as a hunting hook; Loggerheads, local in the summer, prefer posts. In the habit of a songbird they hunt the fields like raptors, impaling prey on barbs of ranching wire. It oscillates with the introduction of the weight, sags at a catenary, and serves as warning to survivors of the species. The birds return to dine, much later, at their leisure.

A terrible ache strikes the miner.

The cochlear vortex has negligible effect on the average vibrational energy of sound waves — the ear would distinguish frequencies just as acutely if it were unrolled as a straight and tapering tube, as in certain reptiles and birds. But the pressure differences detecting lower frequencies are amplified by the spiral form.

With the cochlea expanded to the size of *Spiral Jetty,* the listener would suddenly hear what previously had been unregistered: the infrasound vibrations of trafficked roadways and locomoted tracks, the turbulence of airflow over protuberances of rock at altitude, avalanche, geomagnetic oscillations, storms, the stertorous rhonchus of ventilation in high-volume buildings, compressors and furnaces, movements of crust and magma, imperceptible shifts of tectonic plates — the slap of their collision in the Pacific and the exhalation of their deglutinating separation in the Atlantic — geothermal adjustments to the distribution of subterranean gasses and liquids, blast-furnace operations, construction excavations, mining, the churning of oceans and the chug of rivers, the amatory parley of elephants and the poetry of whales, deglaciations, turbines of container ships, the rush of meteors, productions of lightning, sprites above cumulonimbus clouds, inaudible thundering, the continuous overtones of military aircraft webbing the skies with a Tuuvan throat song, anisotropic fluctuations of the atmosphere itself, the abyssal internal reverberations of metabolism and the deep-sea sonar booms of undercurrent coursing from one's own digestion, respiration, circulation, and excretion. Some of the playback from a *Jetty*-sized phonograph could also be heard.

The listener would be prone to prolonged and profound bouts of headache, doubt, irritation, depression, and fatigue.

Then again, the cochleotropic process might not be intended to amplify low-frequency sounds, as useful as that information is to mammals, but may simply result from the need to avoid the facial nerve and still achieve an efficient packing of the petrous bone.

Calcium carbonate in the vestibular system evinces the mineralization of sensation. Utricles and saccules register acceleration and the lure of gravity — the navigation tools of ancient fishes gift us balance, an echo of their buoyancy and natatory motion now a palpable sense of the planetary ground to which we are bound, having long ago abandoned their thalassic realm. The otoliths are barely audible memories of an ichthyic past. Sensitive to loud, low frequencies as well as ultrasonics, they may provoke a startle reflex from what we cannot consciously hear, giving an acoustic warning of even silent and unheard dangers.

Displaced, these auditory ossicles recreate the sensation of the form of the inner ear: a dizzying spin that sets the world in a vortical rotation as if it were a cochlear cocoon enveloping the modiolar victim of benign paroxysmal vertigo. The small stones recreate a sense of the orbiting earth for which their minerality yearns, aligning us with the planetary mass they insist that we continuously sense, summoning the illusion of a geobiology, in which the terrestrial has been internalized and mimed. All the bones of the human ear furnish a remarkable instance, in fact, of this auditory geology: resonant lithophones arrayed to summon hearing from the sonority of miniature mountain ranges, which wind their spines above flooded valleys.

For a moment, it was perfectly silent. Stansbury stood on deck as the hurricane eye passed directly over his drenched and battered boat — the silence arising not because he was inattentive to the tinnitus hum, or the hint of electrical shimmer from his own neural system, or the resonant reverberations of the ear canal itself registering the low-pressure shift that held the air to the glassy surface of smooth waters, staying for an instant so close that the sea achieved a slight concavity, but because the pattern of the churning vortex, for a split second, perfectly matched the spiral of his inner ear in a silent alignment of form within form.

The conclusion I hoped to reach with this story, with this series of caprices and tocades, was the following: the most dissimilar facts can be connected in such a way that they participate in the same narrative, and their incoherence can become coherent. If you get a call for the wrong number, it's going to rain. If a pigeon alights on the balcony rail, there will be an imminent subway strike. If a territory is renamed, a relative is going to die. There are no restrictions, there are no forbidden subjects, everything is permitted. The whole universe, in its innumerable manifestations, is at your disposal. The only restriction is chance which doesn't really restrict anything because chance, *primum movens*, by definition, is precisely what throws everything, intimate and remote, into communication with one another, short-circuiting and sparking between languages, planes, stories, and details.

This design is now in danger of being frustrated by its myriad details, but in the conduct of this Discourse, I am aiming less at physical than at metaphysical order. If then I seem to step somewhat too discursively from point to point of my topic, let me suggest that I do so in the hope of thus the better keeping unbroken the chain of graduated impressions by which the intellect can expect to encompass the grandeurs of which I speak, and, in their majestic totality, to comprehend them.

Chance is the accident, the clinamenatic swerve of a particle, that kept the universe from being a perfect, undifferentiated block of iron: prill suspends in molten slag, swirling in eddies like the surface of Damascus steel honed sharp as a shark's tooth — the spalled and spent culled as dredge, winnowed in uncouth roughs or rows.

Under the fused spine and foliage of a frond, the radula of *helices aspersa* grasp, and if the ear could hear it would sound like the concert bowing of catgut on antique bass viols.

The needle, caught in a lock groove, clicks the passage of the one-way track with hypnotic nods — a metronome of silence.

Wind continuous with a water wall — the storm, coincident, makes landfall at last.

The final unflexing fold of the map crackles.

The latch, relaxing, gasps, releasing.

Rasping skin passes.

Clock clicks.

Respite.

Tock.

Postface

If the world is still diverse and dynamic, it is because scalability never fulfills its own promises.

— Anna Lowenhaupt Tsing

One's mind and the earth are in a constant state of erosion: mental rivers wear away abstract banks, brain waves undermine cliffs of thought, ideas decompose into stones of unknowing, and conceptual crystallizations break apart into deposits of gritty reason.

— Marga Bijvoet

In April, 1970, Bob Phillips and a small crew from Ogden maneuvered a couple of dump trumps, a front-loader, and a tractor with a grader attachment past the Golden Spike National Historical Monument, over the Class-D Box Elder Country road, to shunt some six-thousand tons of earth and basalt boulders from the hillside shore into the shallow waters of Great Salt Lake, constructing a long groyne, approximately fifteen-feet wide and exactly 1,500 feet long, with a curl at its tip. Robert Smithson, who had conceived of the project, was dissatisfied with the result and had them reconfigure the structure into a tighter coil, spiraling counterclockwise into what would become one of the most iconic works of 20th-century American art.

Not far from Brigham City, past the town of Corinne, the site is often referred to as remote or inaccessible—which might be true if you are in New York, or Los Angeles—but it makes for an easy excursion from Salt Lake City (even quicker, if less fun, in recent years, with the last stretch of rural track signposted, regraded, and cleared of larger rocks and debris). First-time visitors are almost invariably underwhelmed.

Against the distant mountain ranges and the wide horizontal plane of the lake, *Spiral Jetty* looks smaller than expected—particularly after viewers are primed by the remains of a much larger jetty, from an abandoned oil works, passed just before the road rises slightly to offer a first glimpse of Smithson's sculpture. Or rather, a first glimpse in person, after the photographs familiar from any survey of 20th-century art. For many, those images are the only experience of the work available. But visitors, on reflection, realize that the frequently reproduced photographs—shot from the air or carefully framed from the low vantage of a ground's-eye view—often lack any easy referents by which to compare the size of the earthwork. How high up was the helicopter? Is that promontory in the background a low rise or a mountain's foothill? Are we seeing something more like a footpath or a roadway?

The foreshortening of the bouldered slope to the shore is deceiving, to be sure, and once one has walked along the jetty and wound one's way back, retracing, the work's magical ability to transform the sense of space becomes apparent. But it's still not all that big, and despite working with the earth itself, and materials that require heavy-grade construction equipment, Smithson was not building a monumental bulwark. The size of the jetty is far less important than the ways in which it manipulates one's sense of scale. "Size determines an object," Smithson proclaimed in his essay "Spiral Jetty," "but scale determines art," reiterating: "scale is one of the key issues, in terms of art."[1] Nor was Smithson alone in his concern; a couple of years earlier, just

1 Jack Flam, ed., *Robert Smithson: The Collected Writings* (Berkeley: University of California Press, 1996), 147, 211.

as *Spiral Jetty* was completed, Barnett Newman concurred: "size doesn't count. It's scale that counts."[2] Michael Heizer — Smithson's fellow earthwork artist, sometime assistant and sometime rival —echoed the sentiment; when an interviewer used "scale" to refer to the monumentality of "Land Art," Heizer testily policed the same terms: "Not scale, size. Size is real, scale is imagined size." He explained, more thoughtfully, after a moment: "scale could be said to be an aesthetic measurement whereas size is an actual measurement."[3]

Throughout his writings, Smithson evinces not only an interest in scale, but a fascination with its transformations. "A crack in the wall if viewed in terms of scale, not size, could be called the Grand Canyon. A room could be made to take on the immensity of the solar system," he marvels. On the final stop of his "Tour of the Monuments of Passaic, New Jersey," Smithson proposes a similar figuration, imagining a playground sandbox as a "model desert," which then expands even further to encompass an entire, post-apocalyptic planet:

> This monument of minute particles blazed under a bleakly glowing sun, and suggested the sullen dissolution of entire continents, the drying up of oceans — no longer were there green forests and high mountains — all that existed were millions of grains of sand, a vast deposit of bones and stones pulverized into dust.

---

2 Newman continues, dubiously: "It's human scale that counts." Avoiding a pun on *counting* as metrics — the domain of size and not scale — Newman expounds: "and the only way you can achieve human scale is by content." Newman made his statement in a May, 1970 interview with Emile de Antonio for the film *Painters Painting.* Released the same year as the "Spiral Jetty" essay, the "candid history of the New York art scene" caught Smithson's attention and roused his envy; according to Philip Leider, Smithson felt the film had betrayed an entire generation of emerging artists (*Challenging Art: Artforum 1962–1974*, ed. Amy Newman [New York: Soho Press, 2000], 263).

3 Interview with Julia Brown, *Sculpture in Reverse* (Los Angeles: MoCA, 1984).

In the opening phrase of this passage, Smithson tropes William Blake's "minute particulars," a key term in the Romantic writer's visionary poetics. The allusion accounts for the vocabulary of "blazed" and "bleakly," which in turn sum to summon the ghost of *Blake*. As an allegory of its own construction, the text asks its reader to attend to the minute particulars of language in order to reveal the encryption. Specifically, Smithson presumably has in mind the opening of Blake's "Auguries of Innocence": "To see a World in a Grain of Sand/ And a Heaven in a Wild Flower/ Hold Infinity in the palm of your hand/ And Eternity in an hour."[4] But Smithson's allusion goes beyond mere wordplay; Blake's sustained engagement with the aesthetics of the sublime is all to the point.[5] The move from size to scale defines the modern, 18th-century sublime which Blake (and Smithson) will take up and revise. In Immanuel Kant's famous formulation, shifting from size to scale provokes the experience of the sublime. In place of the fixed and non-comparative measure of the "schlechthin groß [absolutely large]" object which, incomparably, "ist eine Größe, die bloß sich selber gleich ist [is a magnitude equal only to itself]," a subjective assessment of relations and a cognitive inability to calculate very large magnitudes produces sublimity. In Smithson's terms, it is the wonderful power by which "you can look at a grain of sand as a gigantic boulder" and from those boulders to a barren planet of calcified mass-extinction.

But what of the move from scale to size? In such an operation — which we might think of as an inversion of the sublime — idealism collapses under the weight of materiality. For Smithson, moreover, such materiality was often linguistic. Smithson glossed "printed matter" as "information which has

---

4 William Blake, *Complete Writings*, ed. Geoffrey Keynes (London: Oxford, 1966), 431.

5 In proximity to that "glowing sun," which might suggest Allen Ginsberg's "Blake-light tragedy" illuminating the "scholars of war" in *Howl*, and the omnicidal "open grave" of pulverized planet that the sandbox becomes, Smithson's line seems to be written under the shadow of the cold-war thermonuclear threat. Smithson and Ginsberg both had William Carlos Williams as their pediatrician.

a kind of physical presence," and he deployed a visual poetics of print materiality in works such as the shaped *A Heap of Language,* the closely-leaded prose of "Strata: a Geophotographic Fiction," and his announcement for a gallery exhibition of "Language to Be Looked at and/or Things to Be Read." Linguistically, the punning we saw with *bleak* and *Blake* also recognizes a material anchoring of abstract ideas, and it was a master trope for *Spiral Jetty.*[6] Smithson's notebooks reveal an interest in salt crystals long before settling on the hypersalinated Great Salt Lake as the site for his construction; even more than its helical shape, salt is a fundamental component of *Spiral Jetty.*[7] When those salt crystals caked, over time, on the rocks that form the jetty, the operative pun emerged; *scale,* as Jennifer Roberts perceptively recognizes, denotes both a hardened, crystalline crust, like the salt on *Spiral Jetty,* as well as a sense of relative proportion.[8] Accordingly, Smithson would have appreciated the famous "éloge du cristal" in André Breton's *L'amour fou*; Breton captions a photograph by Brassaï [Gyula Halász] of enlarged crystals with the wistful reverie: "la maison que j'habite, ma vie, ce que j'écris: je rêve que cela apparaisse de loin comme apparaissent de près ces cubes de sel gemme [the house where I reside, my life, my writing: I dream that all those things might appear from far away like these rock-salt cubes appear from close up]."[9]

Smithson returns to the trope throughout his writing, imagining a planetarium expanding to the size of the universe (an even grander version of that room exploded to the span of the solar-system), and a dot on a map swelling to the limitless horizon.[10] "I'm interested in bringing landscape with low profile up, rather than bringing one with high profile down," Smithson professes, signaling his attraction to deprecated sites: abandoned; indus-

---

6 The pun is an instance of the syzygy discussed below.

7 See Jennifer L. Roberts, *Mirror-Travels: Robert Smithson and History* (New Haven: Yale University Press, 2004), 136.

8 Ibid.

9 André Breton, *L'amour fou* (Paris: Gallimard, 1937), 19.

10 Flam, ed., *Robert Smithson: The Collected Writings,* 27, 94.

trial; *terrains vagues.*[11] However, his preoccupation with rapid and extreme metamorphoses of scale went both ways, not only magnifying the miniscule, but contracting the vast. The original sequence of photographs in his essay "Spiral Jetty," for instance, were carefully orchestrated to form a series of successive close-ups, all the way down to branching salt crystals seen, as in Brassaï's photograph, in extreme closeup.[12] Indeed, like Breton's dialectical image, in which the salt crystals are magnified by the photograph while an entire life is reduced and concentrated to their diminished scale, Smithson imagines his transformations sliding in both directions; "scale inflates or deflates into uneasy dimensions," he writes, leaving us to "wander between the towering and the bottomless. We are lost between the abyss within us and the boundless horizons outside us."[13] Or again: "a point on a map expands to the size of the land mass. A land mass contracts to a point."[14] Aesthetically, the giddy science-fiction surrealism of Smithson's effortlessly scalable contractions and expansions can be exhilarating, and their disorientations are all to the point. As something measurable, size is more or less certain, but scale — for Smithson — is inherently unstable, producing uncertainty, hesitancy, disorientation, and dizziness. Indeed, by predicting that such telescoping reversals of scale provoke "vertigo" [from the Latin *vertere,* to turn], Smithson suggests a spinning akin to the dizzying sensation that can be produced from imbalances within the inner ear, which itself exhibits the vortical structure of the cochlea — a spiral within a spiral, like his sculpture, situated between similar forms in the galactic and molecular realms.

For all its affective power, one should be wary of the frictionless ease and laminar fluidity with which Smithson moves between the molecular and the planetary. This is not the place to mount a detailed critique of nested hierarchical spaces, but

11 Ibid., 297.

12 Roberts, *Mirror-Travels,* 129–30.

13 Flam, ed., *Robert Smithson: The Collected Writings,* 138.

14 Ibid., 153.

I want to gesture toward the problem by reiterating a question posed by Neil Smith, who highlights the politics of scale behind certain conceptual models:

> How do we critically conceive of these various nested scales, how do we arbitrate and translate between them? Furthermore, how do we conceptualize such a translation in a way that centres social practices and politics designed to destroy the oppressive and exploitative intent of hierarchical space?"[15]

Recognizing scale as both a technology and ideology of capitalism, Smith summarizes: "Different societies not only produce space, as [Henri] Lefebvre has taught us, but they also produce scale."[16] In contrast to a unifying hierarchical space, in which everything is subsumed into a single regime of scalabililty, with its attendant privileging of "economies of scale," we might consider not only competing scales, but what they cannot accommodate. For example, both certain modes of capitalism and an understanding of the anthropocenic climate changes that have resulted from those capitalisms require grasping the shifting scales of dynamic interactions; Dipesh Chakrabarty summarizes: "the current conjuncture of globalization and global warming leaves us with the challenge of having to think of human agency over multiple and incommensurable scales at once."[17] Moreover, despite the pleasures of an effortlessly smooth scalability, Anne Lowenhaupt Tsing proposes "a nonscalability theory that pays attention to the mounting pile of ruins that scalability leaves behind." Monuments, Smithson remarked, are "ruins in reverse,"

15 Neil Smith, "Geography, Difference and the Politics of Scale," in *Postmodernism and the Social Sciences,* eds. Joe Doherty, Elspeth Graham, and Mo Malek (New York: Palgrave, 1992), 73.

16 Ibid., 76, 73.

17 Dipesh Chakrabarty, "Postcolonial Studies and the Challenge of Climate Change," *New Literary History* 43, no. 1 (2012): 1. For a further analysis of this intellectual confluence, see Christopher Nealon, "Infinity for Marxists," *Mediations: Journal of the Marxist Literary Group* 28, no. 2 (Spring 2015): 47–64.

and despite his eager and easy scalar moves we might still locate in his aesthetics the grounds for a nonscalability theory that "makes it possible to see how scalability uses articulations with nonscalable forms even as it denies or erases them."[18]

Size—which may not matter but always implicates matter—is objective. Scale, in contrast, is a matter of perception and politics. But the material specificity of size provides a pivot-point against which to counter the ideological abstractions of political systems. Smithson offers a telling anecdote about the federal regulation requiring mining operations to refill any excavations they make:

> You can imagine the result when they try to deal with the Bingham pit in Utah which is a pit one mile deep and three miles across. Now the idea of the law being so general and not really dealing with a specific site like that seems unfortunate.[19]

Having demolished an entire mountaintop, just across the lake from *Spiral Jetty*, the Bingham canyon mine would essentially have to replicate its devastation—displacing the equivalent of yet another mountain peak (over ten cubic kilometers of earth), with Sisyphean absurdity—in order to fulfill its obligations to environmental aesthetics under the politics of reclamation. Moreover, form may scale readily, but the forces that act on the materials in question do not. A replica of the open pit mine, for instance, might look identical to the actual site, but the weight of the material under gravity will give a very different risk of slope collapse at different sizes, with different soil types, in different temperatures, and so on.

Furthermore, equivalence across scales, paradoxically, obviate our ability to register scale itself. With his photo-illustrations

18 Anna Lowenhaupt Tsing, "On Nonscalability: The Living World Is Not Amenable to Precision-Nested Scales," *Common Knowledge* 18, no. 3 (Fall 2012): 506.

19 Flam, ed., *Robert Smithson: The Collected Writings*, 307.

and filmic montage, Smithson exacerbates an ocular condition that is always the case. Following Davis Summers's argument that "abstraction from size is a fundamental operation of vision," Jennifer Roberts concludes: "scale, quite simply, is difficult to see."[20] The difficulty arises from a "scalar elasticity at the core of visual perception":"a physiological condition according to which "the eye and its lensing operations inherently rescale all objects, breaking them out of their real material extent and re-presenting them at a different size."[21] In the present moment of networked graphic interfaces, the phone or computer screen compounds this decoupling of material and representation with dynamic or preset rescaling and magnification and then further constrains the visualization of any and all data by the fixed width of a pixel screen.

The specific particularity of size against the abstraction of a system can be clearly seen in Marcel Duchamp's spoof of the *mètre des archives,* which since 1889 had set the distance between two marks on an alloyed bar (of 90% platinum and 10% iridium, at the temperature of the melting point of ice, to be precise).[22] To produce his *3 stoppages-étalons* [*3 Invisible Mending Stitches Made Visible*] (1914), Duchamp supposedly held a meter-long string — horizontally taut — one meter above the ground, and allowed it to fall freely; the chance curve of the string when it landed was then taken as the template for a precisely-tooled measuring stick. The procedure was repeated to yield three wooden rulers, none of which are the same linear length but all of which wend the same distance along their variously curved extensions. As instruments, they could only ever be used to

20 Jennifer L. Roberts, *Scale* (Chicago: University of Chicago Press, 2016), 12.
21 Ibid.
22 The meter in France had originally been set in 1790 as a fraction of the distance from the equator to the north pole along the path passing through Paris; after the archived bar was abandoned in 1960, the meter was subsequently redefined in terms of the wavelengths in a vacuum as a filament of Krypton-86 is radiated to the transition between the quantum atomic energy levels 2p10 and 5d5; it currently reflects the distance that light travels in a vacuum during a fraction (1/299,792,458) of a second, as measured by a Cesium-133 atomic clock.

measure the unique, arbitrary singularity of the curved string they record.

That chance curve of a falling object recalls Lucretius' "clinamen": "the slight swerve made by a primal atom at some unknown place and time [facit exiguum clinamen principiorum nec regione loci certa nec tempore certo]" as it falls otherwise straight downward through space:

> corpora cum deorsum rectum per inane feruntur ponderibus propriis, incerto tempore ferme incertisque locis spatio depellere paulum, tantum quod momen mutatum dicere possis

> while bodies are being pulled downward by their own weight, in a straight path through the void, at uncertain moments and uncertain places they swerve slightly from their course, just enough so you could say you discern a change of motion.[23]

Alfred Jarry, a direct influence on Duchamp, would take up Lucretius's clinamen as a *terme de métier* of his aesthetic philosophy in order to figure an exception, the subject of his new science of 'pataphysics. In the famous definition given in *Gestes et opinions du docteur Faustroll, pataphysicien,* Jarry (ventriloquizing through his title character) declared:

> La pataphysique sera surtout la science du particulier [...]. Elle étudiera les lois qui régissent les exceptions, et expliquera l'univers supplémentaire à celui-ci; ou moins ambitieusement décrira un univers que l'on peut voir et que peut-être l'on doit voir à la place du traditionnel [...].

23 Lucretius, *De Rerum Naturam / On the Nature of Things,* Loeb Classical Library 181 (Cambridge: Harvard University Press, 1924), Bk. II, ll. 292–93, 217–20.

> DÉFINITION.—La pataphysique est la science des solutions imaginaires, qui accorde symboliquement aux linéaments les propriétés des objets décrits par leur virtualité
>
> Pataphysics will be, above all, the science of the particular [...]. It will investigate the laws that govern exceptions, and it will explain the universe supplementary to this one; or, less ambitiously, it will describe a universe that one can envision — and that perhaps one must envision — in place of the traditional one [...].
>
> DEFINITION: Pataphysics is the science of imaginary solutions, which symbolically attributes to their lineaments the properties of objects described by their virtuality.[24]

We know that Smithson was reading Jarry while planning *Spiral Jetty.* In his "Metamorphosis of the Spiral," a set of working notes for the project, Smithson transcribed a line from *Faustroll*: "For, just as Professor Cayley recorded the past in the two dimensions of a black surface [of the mathematician's chalkboard], so the progress of the solid future entwined the body in spirals."[25] The text would have been available to Smithson in the Grove Press *Selected Works,* which had been published in 1965, edited

24 Alfred Jarry, *Gestes et opinions du docteur Faustroll, pataphysicien: Roman néoscientifique* (Paris: Charpentier, 1911), 30-31.

25 Reproduced in Lynne Cooke and Karen Kelly with Bettins Funcke and Barbara Schröder, eds., *Robert Smithson: Spiral Jetty* (New York and Berkeley: DIA Foundation and University of California Press, 2005), 135.

In a 1964 lecture at the City Art Museum (St. Louis), Duchamp related his stoppages to pataphysics (see Herbert Molderings, *Duchamp and the Aesthetics of Chance: Art as Experiment* [New York: Columbia University Press, 2010], 83). Nico Israel implicitly associates Smithson and Jarry by including them in the company of modernists such as Beckett, Joyce, and Duchamp who also exploited the iconography of the spiral; see *Spirals: The Whirled Image in Twentieth-Century Literature and Art* (New York: Columbia University Press, 2015); Edward A. Shanken explicitly argues for recognizing the connection between Smithson and Jarry in "Broken Circle &/ Spiral Hill? Smithson's Spirals, Pataphysics, Syzygy and Survival," *Technoetic Arts: A Journal of Speculative Research* 11, no. 1 (2013): 3–14.

by Roger Shattuck. A few years earlier, Shattuck had also edited a special issue of *The Evergreen Review*, the flagship disseminator of the avant-garde in America at the time. Subtitled *What Is 'Pataphysics?*, the issue's cover crops a striking, hand-drawn, purple spiral over a green ground.[26] The chromatic schema was reversed for the Grove Press book-cover design, with a green spiral on the blue back cover and a green-tinted print of Jarry's woodblock portrait of his character King Ubu—the spiral *gidouille* on his torso prominently displayed. In contemplating a similar spiral, to be built on some saline lake, Smithson might have been taken by another sentence in Jarry's neo-scientific novel describing the unspooling of a spiral form (underscoring the *roll* in *Faust<u>roll</u>*): "the wallpaper of Faustroll's body was unrolled by the saliva and teeth of the water [le papier de tenture se déroulait, sous la salive et les dents de l'eau]."[27]

Smithson, given to reversals and the swings between "the towering and the bottomless," might also have been struck by the book's query: "rather than state the law of falling bodies toward a center, why do we not phrase it as the rise of the void toward a periphery [au lieu d'énoncer la loi de la chute des corps vers un centre, que ne préfère-t-on celle de l'ascension du vide vers une périphérie]?"[28] Here, amid a scene of the Lucretian rain of atoms, Jarry figures what he termed *syzygy*. An astronomical term describing the conjunction or opposition of planets in a solar system, syzygy might have appealed to Smithson for the same reason Shattuck suspected it appealed to Jarry: "because it suggests that something akin to crystalline form may emerge at intervals out of the random movements of the cosmos."[29] Transposed to other realms, the figure generates symmetrical relations transfixed through a conjunction of otherwise opposing bodies along an unexpected axis, giving a formal structure to abstractly conceptual dynamic and reifying relations into

26 *Evergreen Review* 4, no. 14 (May–June 1960).
27 Jarry, *Gestes et opinions du docteur Faustroll, pataphysicien*, 105.
28 Ibid., 22.
29 Alfred Jarry, *Selected Works*, ed. Roger Shattuck (New York: Grove Press, 1965), xvii.

figures or forms.[30] Where the clinamen disrupts the order of things, the syzygy doubles down on exceptions by linking two singularities in a single, fixed form.[31] Smithson, as Marjorie Perloff recognizes, "was always drawn to dialectical propositions," an insight elaborated by Roberts, who discovers the dialectical valence of salt itself in Smithson's constructions.[32] Along the entire chain of fractal analogues in his rhetoric of spirals, from the galaxy on down to the microscopic structure of the sodium chloride crystals, where "each cubic salt crystal echoes the *Spiral Jetty* in terms of the crystal's molecular lattice," Smithson proposed that "all of the things internally have that [same] aspect, they are all involved with the unification of the duplicity, the dual aspect is reconciled within the pieces, and reflects a greater scale of the dialectic."[33]

Dialectics, however, are honed on concrete particulars, just as scale is tested by size. *Helicology*, accordingly, undertakes an investigation of the limits of scale through a pataphysical narrative about Smithson's *Spiral Jetty* [where *about* retains its etymology from the Old English *onbutan*: around the circumference, with a rotating or spiraling motion]. It is a work of experimental fiction, where "experimental" is understood in its scientific sense and where the narrative elements of science — from the pre-socratics to the quantum theorists of Jarry's day — have not been forgotten. In Lucretius's natural science, the implications of clinamina accounted for the myriad variations perceptible in the universe; they explained why the world was not a perfectly uniform block of undifferentiated matter (and they set up a

30 See Johanna Drucker, *SpecLab: Digital Aesthetics and Projects in Speculative Computing* (Chicago: University of Chicago Press, 2009), 103.

31 As Steve McCaffery puts it: "if the clinamen disturbs the laws of nature, then syzygy reinforces those laws pertaining to exceptions, for it brings about a confraternity of two anomalies." Steve McCaffery, *The Darkness of the Present: Poetics, Anachronism, and the Anomaly* (Tuscaloosa: University of Alabama Press, 2012), 170.

32 Marjorie Perloff, *The Futurist Moment: Avant-Garde, Avant Guerre, and the Language of Rupture* (Chicago: University of Chicago Press, 1987), 232; Roberts, *Mirror-Travels*, 137.

33 Flam, ed., *Robert Smithson: The Collected Writings*, 239.

miniature material drama of the conundrum of chance and free will that would continue to haunt later philosophers). In Jarry's speculative science, on the other hand, they hinted at a certain utopian politics ('pataphysics, recall, would describe the world that one *must* [*doit*] envision in place of the status quo); here the geometric revolution of the spiral and the political revolution of society coincide — a conjunction that we might also glimpse in the clinaminatic swerve of the Situationist *dérive* [drift].

For both Lucretius and Jarry, the new path of the veering atom, however absurd, was subsequently followed ineluctably once it had been made. The deviation from the plumb might not be predictable or accountable by the laws of physics, but once on its new trajectory the particle and its interactions within the atomic system conformed to all the usual deterministic laws of mechanics — until further clinamina intervened. Similarly, an imaginary solution might begin with an error, but it follows through with a relentless, deadpan, exhaustive precision. Pataphysics takes the grammatical form of *as if*; it suspends disbelief so as to concentrate on the consequences and ramifications of an initial swerve with focused concentration and all the seriousness of young children at play.[34] Duchamp's *stoppages,* for instance, are patently absurd experiments, producing useless rules and worthless guides, but those instruments are machined with precision and stored in a bespoke case with reverent care. His "joke about the meter," as he glossed the piece, may seem glib, but the blague is carried out with earnest patience and without cracking a smile.[35] In his notes, Duchamp referred to the *trois stoppages-étalons* as "hasard en conserve [canned chance]," an

34 Cf. aphorism §94: "Reife des Mannes: Das heißt, den Ernst wiedergefunden zu haben, den man als Kind hatte, beim Spie [A man's maturity—consists in having found again the seriousness one had as a child at play]." Friedrich Nietzsche, *Jenseits von Gut und Böse: Vorspiel einer Philosophie der Zukunft* (Leipzig: C. G. Naumann, 1886), 91; *Beyond Good and Evil: Prelude to a Philosophy of the Future,* trans. Walter Kaufmann (New York: Vintage, 1966), 83.

35 Duchamp makes the statement on the acquisition questionnaire administered by the museum; see Molderings, *Duchamp and the Aesthetics of Chance,* 83.

archival preservation of the aleatoric swerve, extending its shelf-life through a conservation of its consequences.

Helicology—a work that seeks to maintain the power of *Spiral Jetty* by applying a torque to its angular velocity—similarly attempts to follow through on Smithson's initial swerve by tracking the implications of the formal equivalences he invites us to make in the triangulated, eponymous sites of earthwork, film, and essay. Paradoxically, entertaining the shifts in scale proposed by Smithson's jetties culminates in the cancellation of scale, which is abolished by equivalence. Within the dizzying elasticity of Smithson's imagination, I try to locate a scalar specificity that might counter the hyperscalability of our cultural moment.[36] *Helicology* calculates materials with a pataphysical ingenuousness, and in the process of demonstrating its imaginary solution discovers that materiality always annuls those abstractions that would seek to contain, organize, or comprehend the real. Solutions, by definition, only occur when something has been dissolved.

Then again, it is also a clock. The time it takes to read *Helicology* out loud equals the time it takes to drive to *Spiral Jetty* from the house where I reside. As it recedes, in the rearview mirror, it appears to be like cubes of sodium chloride seen close up. "Objects in mirror are closer than they appear," the text superimposed on the world promises and warns. On the return, the crystal encrustations on the lake bed shimmer into the halated glare of what I write. In both cases, I mainly see a film of aluminum behind the mirage. But the timing is precise. It is a pleasantly short ride or an awfully long way, depending on your sense of scale.

36 See Roberts, "Seeing Scale," 15.

Quotations, Allusions, and Deformations

xv

Inside some stones: Roger Caillois, *L'écriture des pierres* (Paris: Flammarion, 1970), 94–95.

xvii

Size determines: Robert Smithson, "The Spiral Jetty," in *Robert Smithson: The Collected Writings*, ed. Jack Flam (Berkeley: University of California Press, 1996), 147.

23

a beautiful machine of peculiar construction: "When we trace the parts of which this terrestrial system is composed, and when we view the general connection of those several parts, the whole presents a machine of peculiar construction by which it is adapted to a certain end." James Hutton, address to the Royal Society of Edinburg, March 7, 1785, *Transactions of the Royal Societry of Edinburgh,* Vol. I (Edinburgh: J. Dickson, 1788), 209.

bending and breaking off and melting: Ludwig Wittgenstein, *Remarks on the Foundations of Mathematics*, eds. G.H.

von Wright and Rush Rhees, trans. G.E.M. Anscombe (Cambridge: MIT Press, 1967), 122.

24

Parkinson & Frodsham: Captain J.H. Simpson, *Report of Explorations Across the Great Basin off the Territory of Utah* (Washington, DC: Government Printing Office, 1876), 162.

soft-cushioned, et seq.: Ibid., 160–61.

callis sand — reddish and suspended in the water: Martin Lister, "An Ingenious Proposal for a new sort of Maps of Countrys, together with Tables of Sands and Clays, such chiefly as are found in the North parts of England, drawun up about 10 years since, and delievered to the Royal Society March 12, 1683," *Philosophical Transactions, Giving Some Accompt of the Present Undertakings, Studies, and Labours, of the Ingenious in Many Considerable Parts of the World,* Vol. XIV (Oxford: Moses Pitt, 1684), 737.

25

siren twist: "torsion de sirène." Stéphane Mallarmé, *Un coup de dés jamais n'abolira le hazard* (Paris: Gallimard, 1914), n.p.

red alluvium of strife: Roy Campbell, "Poets in Africa," in *The Calendar of Modern Letters,* Vols. 3–4, eds. Edgell Rickword and Douglas Garman (London: Frank Cass, 1926), 128.

unable to distinguish: Robert Smithson, "Visible," in *Robert Smithson: The Collected Writings,* ed. Flam, 302.

light from water: Rosalind Krauss, "Entropy," in *Formless: A User's Guide,* eds. Yves-Alain Bois and Rosalind Krauss (New York: Zone Books, 1997), 73.

the mirror kept changing places with the reflection: Robert Smithson, "A Tour of the Monuments of Passaic, New Jersey," in *Robert Smithson: The Collected Writings,* ed. Flam, 73.

structural blindness: Krauss, "Entropy," 77.

all boundaries and distinctions lost their meanings in an ocean of slate, the present falling backward into a petrified sea:

Robert Smithson, "A Sedimentation of the Mind: Earth Projects," in *Robert Smithson: The Collected Writings*, ed. Flam, 110.

sun has turned to glass: Robert Smithson, "Tour," in *Robert Smithson: The Collected Writings*, ed. Flam, 72.

glide of purely optical movement: Krauss, "Entropy," 75.

the crystal is the seat of greater disorder than its parent liquid: Percy W. Bridgman, *The Nature of Thermodynamics* (Gloucester: P. Smith, 1969), 175.

the future will have been forgotten: Robert Smithson, "Entropy and the New Monuments," in *Robert Smithson: The Collected Writings*, ed. Flam, 15.

the strata of so many forgotten books: Robert Smithson, "A Provisional Theory of Non-sites," in *Robert Smithson: The Collected Writings*, ed. Flam, xxv.

maps, charts, advertisements, art books, science books, money, architectural plans, math books, graphs, diagrams, newspapers, comics, booklets and pamphlets from industrial companies: Robert Smithson, "The Crystal Land," in *Robert Smithson: The Collected Writings*, ed. Flam, 18.

gaudy prints, passé literature, church Latin, erotica full of spelling errors, novels our grandmothers loved, fairy tales, little children's books, old operas: "enluminures populaires; la littérature démodée, latin d'église, livres érotiques sans orthographe, romans de nos aïeules, contes de fées, petits livres de l'enfance, opéras vieux." Arthur Rimbaud, "Alchimie du verbe," in *Oeuvres complètes* (Paris: Gallimard, 1954), 232.

leaflets, papers, cards, circulars, etc.: *Oxford English Dictionary*, "printed-matter," s.v. "printed."

26

by means of a snail: William Carpenter, *Mechanical Philosophy, Horology, and Astronomy* (London: Wm. S. Orr and Co., 1843), 379; cf. "The rack has four teeth, corresponding with the four steps of the snail" (ibid., 363–64).

its noonday: Steven Hirsch and Lucien van der Walt, eds., *Anarchism and Syndicalism in the Colonial and Postcolonial World, 1870–1940* (Leiden: Brill, 2010).

27

time machines: "Une bonne ouvrière ne fait avec le fuseau que cinq mailles à la minute, certaine métiers circulaires à tricoter en font trente mille dans le même temps. Chaque minute à la machine équivaut donc à cent heures de travail de l'ouvrière; ou bien chaque minute de travail de la machine deliver à l'ouvrière dix jours de repos [A good working woman makes with her needles only five meshes a minute, while certain circular knitting machines make 30,000 in the same time. Every minute of the machine is thus equivalent to a hundred hours of the workingwomen's labor, or again, every minute of the machine's labor, gives the working women ten days of rest]." Paul Lafargue, *Le droit à la paresse* (Paris: Éditions Allia, 2005), 36–37 / *The Right to Be Lazy and Other Studies,* trans. Charles H. Kerr (Chicago: Charles Kerr & Co. Cooperative, 1907), 31.

28

Bob Phillips: Smithson, "The Spiral Jetty," 146.

principle of levers, et seq.: R. McNeill Alexander, *Dynamics of Dinosaurs and Other Extinct Giants* (New York: Columbia University Press, 1989), 67.

Cold War: *Soviet Education* 16 (1973): 25. The figure should not be confused with the 70,000 Newtons that Apple computers sold within the line's first few months on the market (*Information Week* [1997], 86).

F-111A: NTSB-AAR-75-12 Report (1975).

main engine: *Space World* (1980), 40; Eric G. Swedin, "Utah's Spaceport: A Failed Dream," *Utah Historical Quarterly* 84, no. 3 (Summer 2016): 260–61; see Raymond L. Hixson, "Confidential Report to Spaceport Committee," March 22, 1971 (self-published).

train car: Chuanhe He, *Deformation Controllable Bogie Impact Structure Design*, M.Sc. Thesis, University of California at Davis, 1989, 9.

29

revolving screen: John S. Watts, "Estimating the Horsepower Required to Drive Machinery," *American Machinist* 54, no. 18 (May 5, 1921): 792–93.

twenty-five pounds of coal: Harry Kitsikopoulos, *Innovation and Technological Diffusion: An Economic History of Early Steam Engines* (Oxford: Routledge, 2016), 143, 115.

Assyrian temple: "Babylonian Brick," *The Clay-Worker* 43–44 (1905): 251.

Dravidian languages: Vishnupriya Kolipakam et al., "A Bayesian Phylogenetic Study of the Dravidian Language Family," *Royal Society Open Science* 5, no. 3 (2018).

Alerka: *Popular Science Monthly* 20 (1881): 402.

30

oceanic-tidal cycles: Charles D. Keeling and Timothy P. Whorf, "The 1,800-year Oceanic Tidal Cycle: A Possible Cause of Rapid Climate Change," *Proceedings of the National Academy of Sciences of the United States of America* 97–98 (2000): 3814–19.

rhyolitic tephra: P.C. Froggait, "Motutere Tephra Formation and Redefinition of Hinemaiaia Tephra Formation, Taupo Volcanic Centre, New Zealand," *New Zealand Journal of Geology and Geophysics* 24, no. 1 (1981): 99–105.

31

the resort of sea birds: James Hingston Tuckey, *Maritime Geography and Statistics, Or: a Description of the Ocean and its Coasts, Maritime Commerce, Navigation, &c. &c. &c.*, Vol. V (London: Black, Parry, and Co., 1815), 551; *The Gazetteer of Scotland; containing A Particular Description of the Counties, Parishes, Islands, Cities, Towns, Villages, Lakes, Rivers, Mountains, Vallies, &c. in That Kingdom: with a descriptive sketch of the country, its extent and boundaries, a table of the population, and a correct table of the principal roads, With An Elegant Map*, 2nd edn. (Edinburgh: Archibald Constable and Company, 1806), s.v. "dungisbay-head."

fallen, transported: Loren Eiseley, *The Firmament of Time* (New York: Athaneum. 1966), 10.

now extirpated species: Junius Henderson and L.E. Daniels, "Hunting Mollusca in Utah and Idaho," *Proceedings of the Academy of Natural Sciences of Philadelphia* 68, no. 3 (May–June 1916): 322 et seq.; Ralph V. Chamberlin and David T. Jones, "A Descriptive Catalog of the Mollusca of Utah," *Bulletin of the University of Utah* 19, no. 4 (1929): 47; David Tracy Jones, "A Study of the Great Basin Land Snail: Oreohelix strigosa depressa," *Bulletin of the University of Utah* 31, no. 4, Biological Series 6, no. 1 (1940); George V. Oliver and William R. Bosworth III, *Rare, Imperiled, and Recently Extinct or Extirpated Mollusks of Utah: A Literature Review* (Salt Lake City: Utah Division of Wildlife Resources, 1999), 180; George V. Oliver and William R. Bosworth III, "Oreohelices of Utah, I. Rediscovery of the Uinta mountain snail, Oreohelix eurekensis uinta Brooks, 1939 (Stylommatophora Oreohelicidae)," *Western North American Naturalist* 60, no. 4 (2000): 454.

the jumble of various grains: see "the snail […] began to labour over the crumbs of loose earth which broke away and rolled down as it passed over them. It appeared to have a definite goal in front of it" (Virginia Woolf, "Kew Gardens," in *Monday or Tuesday* [New York: Harcourt, Brace and Company, 1921], 87); "the grey-shelled snail draws across the path and flattens the blades behind him" (Virginia Woolf, *The Waves* [London: The Hogarth Press, 1931], 9).

32

the speed of snails: "we think that size does not have anything to do with the snail's speed and movement." Qtd. in Peter Shaw, *Science* (New York: Citation Press, 1972), 18.

Pliocene deposits: L.C. Bortz, "Heavy-Oil Deposit, Great Salt Lake, Utah," in *Exploration for Heavy Crude Oil and Natural Bitumen*, AAPG Studies in Geology 25, ed. Richard F. Meyer (Tulsa: American Association of Petroleum Geologists, 1987); John W. Hosterman, Richard F. Meyer, Curtis A. Palmer, Michael W. Doughten, and Donald E. Anders, "Chemistry and Mineralogy of Natural Bitumens and Heavy Oils and Their Reservoir Rocks from the United States, Canada, Trinidad and Tobago, and Venezuela," *U.S. Geological Survey Circular* 1047 (1990): 18.

33

ruffe: Joshua Sylvester, "Iob Triumphant," trans. of Guillaume Salluste Du Bartas' *Diuine Weekes & Works* (1605), 921.

and if a horned diuell: John Marston, *Antonios reuenge: The second part. As it hath beene sundry times acted, by the children of Paules* (London: Bradock, 1602), Scena Tertia, line 10.

two cranes: Philemon Holland, trans., *Pliny's Natural History: A Selection* (Oxford: Clarendon, 1964), 110.

spotless and sombre egrets: Gracius Joseph Broinowski, "Herodias Melanopus and Herodias Asha," in *The Birds of Australia*, Vol. II (Melbourne: Charles Stuart & Co., 1891), pl. XIX.

35

all distance: Institute of Contemporary Art, *Theatergarden Bestiarium: The Garden as Theater as Museum*, ed. Chris Dercon (Long Island City: P.S.1, 1999).

in a long race of vertuous Ancestors: Ben Jonson, *Catiline His Conspiracy* (London: Burre, 1611), Act iij.

36

rakes the saddle: *Rendezvous: Idaho State University Journal of Arts and Letters* 19–21 (1983): 35.

37

subsurface traces: Max Crittenden, "Bedrock Geologic Map of the Promontory Mountains, Box Elder County, Utah," *USGS Open-File Report* 88–646 (1988).

bells: "Other misunderstandings resulted from the names applied to the organ. For the rattle or rattle lobes, the earliest accounts used the Spanish cascabel (Cirça, 1554) and the Portuguese term cascavel (Magalhães de Gandavo, 1576, fol 24r) meaning 'a small bell'; so it is not strange that an early English report (Purchas, 1614, p. 842) should refer to the snake 'which hath a bell in his tayle,' or that one of the first Latin descriptions (Piso, 1648, p.41) should use the term tintinabuli, meaning bells. Thus we have several early reports likening the sound of the rattle to that of bells or cymbals." Laurence Monroe Klauber, *Rattlesnakes: Their Habits, Life Histories, and Influence on Mankind,* Vol. 1 (San Diego: Zoological Society of San Diego, 1997), 270.

corn in granary: Jill D. Greer, "Baxoje-Jiwere Grammar Sketch," in *Advances in the Study of Siouan Languages and Linguistics,* eds. Catherine Rudin and Bryan Gordon (Berlin: Language Science Press, 2016), 212.

38

avis: Latin "bird"; Old French: "warning," from *aviser*: *a* [prefix: to direct toward] + *viser* [to see].

keratoid: Klauber, *Rattlesnakes,* 295.

39

oldsquaw: *Annual Narrative Report* (Brigham City: Bear River Migratory Bird Refuge, 1992), 19.

burning surge of perpetual heat: *Isidore of Seville's Etymologies: The Complete English Translation of Isidori Hispalensis Episcopi Etymologiarum sive Originum Libri XX,* trans. Priscilla Throop (Charlotte: Medieval MS, 2005), XII 4.5.

the ground strewn with cindered fragments: Howard Stansbury, *An Expedition to the Valley of the Great Salt Lake of Utah: Including A Description of its Geography, Natural History,*

And Minerals, and an Analysis of Its Waters: With an Authentic Account of the Mormon Settlement (Philadelphia: Lippincott, Grambo & Co., 1852), 266.

Streaked and puddled with oil: Mary Ann Gwinn, "Mournful Cry of a Loon Still Echoes Long after Exxon Valdez Has Gone," *The Seattle Times,* March 24, 1999.

xeric scrub: Brooke Arkush and Bonnie Pitblados, "Paleoarchaic Surface Assemblages in the Great Salt Lake Desert, Northwestern Utah," *Journal of California and Great Basin Anthropology* 22, no. 1 (2000): 12–42; George T. Jones et al., "Lithic Source Use and Paleoarchaic Foraging Territories in the Great Basin," *American Antiquity* 68, no. 1 (Jan. 2003); Ann Cornell, Mark Stuart, and Steven Simms, "An Obsidian Cache from the Great Salt Lake Wetlands, Weber County, Utah," *Utah Archaeology* 5, no. 1 (1992), 154–58.

40

white quartz, and blood-red jasper: Stansbury, *An Expedition to the Valley of the Great Salt Lake of Utah,* 266.

weird and commanding beauty: Edward Sullivan, *The Book of Kells: Described by Sir Edward Sullivan, Bart., And Illustrated with Twenty-Four Plates in Colours,* 2nd edn. (London: The Studio, 1920), 1.

In Stansbury's time, a rattlesnake was thought to strike two-thirds its length: "Hogg (1928, p. 53) and MacDonald (1946, p. 135) give the maximum striking distance as 1/3 of the snake's length; Kalm (1752–53, p. 54), Carver (1799, p. 484), and Weld (1800, p. 409) at 1/2; Audobon (1827, p. 26) and Notestein (1905, p. 120) at 2/3; and finally Dudley (1723, p. 292), Odmixon (1741, Vol. I, p. 188), Wesley (1784, vol. 2, p. 37), and Cigne (1832, p. 90) considered that a snake might strike up to its own length." Klauber, *Rattlesnakes,* 482.

41

Chokia mound: Lynda Norene Shaffer, *Native Americans Before 1492: The Moundbuilding Centers of the Eastern Woodlands* (Armonk: M.E. Sharpe, 1992), 51.

outer curtain wall: Kenneth M. Setton and Harry W. Hazard, eds., *A History of the Crusades, Volume Four: The Art and Architecture of the Crusader States* (Madison: University of Wisconsin Press, 1977), 214.

Duluth, South Shore: John W. Jochim, ed., *Michigan and Its Resources: Sketches of the Growth of the State, Its Industries, Agricultural Productions, Institutions, And Means of Transportation; Descriptions of its Soil, Climate, Timber, Financial Condition, and the Situation of its Unoccupied Lands; and a Review of Its General Characteristics As a Home* (Lansing: Robert Smith & Co., 1893), 129.

B&O warehouse: Herbert Harwood, *Impossible Challenge* (Baltimore: Bernard, Roberts and Co., 1979), 150.

Gatun locks: Freederik Nebeker, *Dawn of the Electronic Age: Electrical Technologies in the Shaping of the Modern World: 1914–1945* (Hoboken: John Wiley & Sons, 2009), 1.

Eureka Creek: Henry Gannett, *The Origin of Certain Place Names in the United States*, 2nd edn., USGS Bulletin No. 258, Series F (Washington, DC: Government Printing Office, 1905), 117.

Stewart J. Cort: Raymond Bawal, *Superships of the Great Lakes* (Clinton Township: Inland Expressions, 2011), 9–11.

long-vanished Ice-Age glacier: *Frommer's Guide: Things to See in Drenthe* (Hoboken: Wiley, 2020).

great sand dunes: Stephen Trimble, *Great Sand Dunes National Monument: The Shape of the Wind* (Tucson: Western National Parks Association, 2000), 12.

42

garden spider's thread: *Transactions of the Society for the Encouragement of Arts, Manufacture, and Commerce* XLVIII (London, 1831), 235.

reeling yield of a silkworm: Gideon B. Smith, "The Filature, Reeling Silk, &c.," *Journal of the American Silk Society and Rural Economist* 1, no. 5 (May 1839): 161.

fairy-spire: William Makepeace Thayer, *Marvels of the New West: A Vivid Portrayal of the Stupendous Marvels in the Vast Wonderland West of the Missouri River* (Norwich: Henry Bill, 1887), 161.

Quelccaya Ice Cap…Ogallala aquifer: Bruce Elliott Johansen, *The Encyclopedia of Global Warming Science and Technology* (Santa Barbara: Greenwood, 2009), 37; John Opie, "Ecology and Environment," in *The Great Plains Region,* ed. Amanda Rees (Westport: Greenwood, 204), 88; Francis J. Monkhouse, *Principles of Physical Geography* (Plymouth: Rowman & Littlefield, 1964), 138.

soft hematite: Lucien Eaton, "Mining Soft Hematite at Mine No. 2 of the Marquette Range, Michigan," *Information Circular* #6179 (Department of Commerce, Bureau of Mines, October, 1929), 6.

dredged in a day: Kristine L. Bradof, "Ditching of Red Lake Peatland During the Homestead Era," in *The Patterned Peatlands of Minnesota,* eds. Herbett Edgar Wright, Barbara Coffin, and Norman Asseng (Minneapolis: University of Minnesota Press, 1992), 265.

rolling sugar cane: *Document in Relation to the Prevention of Explosions of Steam Boilers,* 25th Congress, 3rd Session, 217 (1839), 4.

bacon: Endel Karmas, *Meat Product Manufacture* (Park Ridge: Noyes Data Corp, 1970), 198.

Governor Connally's wrist: Larry M. Sturdivan, *The JFK Myths: A Scientific Investigation of the Kennedy Assassination* (St. Paul: Paragon House, 2005), 144.

biggest oil tanker: David Chance, *Around the World in 80 Years* (n.p.: Xlibris, 2012), 129.

Croton River dam: William Garnett, *A Little Book on Water Supply* (Cambridge: Cambridge University Press, 1922), 44.

43

We may be best served: Katherine T. Jones, "Scale as Epistemology," *Political Geography* 17, no. 8 (1998): 28.

snakespiral springs: James Joyce, *Ulysses* (New York: Vintage, 1961), 731. On Joyce and spirals more generally, see Nico Israel, *Spirals: The Whirled Image in Twentieth-Century Literature and Art* (New York: Columbia University Press, 2015), 139–60.

44

recovery of scrap copper: Nicholas Georgescu-Roegen, *Entropy Law and the Economic Process* (Cambridge: Harvard University Press, 1971), 278–80.

electrolytic copper: Adam Minter, *Junkyard Planet: Travels in a Billion Dollar Trash Trade* (New York: Bloomsbury, 2013), Chapter 8.

45

"Notes to Aid": Alfred Jarry, "Commentaire pour servir à la construction pratique de la machine à explorer le temps," *Le Mercure de France* 110 (February 1899): 387–96.

projector…is the time machine: Smithson, "The Spiral Jetty," 150.

48

crystallography, in turn, leads to mapmaking: Robert Smithson, "Discussion with Heizer, Oppenheim, Smithson," in *Robert Smithson: The Collected Writings*, ed. Flam, 244.

the cone opens wide: Emily Dickinson, *Emily Dickinson's Poems: As She Preserved Them*, ed. Christanne Miller (Cambridge: Harvard University Press, 2016), 233.

49

under the gaze of those crazed pneumatic clocks: "sous l'oeil des horloges pneumatiques affolées." Robert Desnos, *Nouvelles Hébrides et autres textes, 1922–1930* (Paris: Gallimard, 1978), 36.

50

Port Authority: Robert Sullivan, "The Source of Robert Smithson's Spiral," *The New Yorker,* June 18, 2014, https://www.newyorker.com/culture/culture-desk/the-source-of-robert-smithsons-spiral.

a vertical cylinder of shattered and altered monzonite: *Geological Survey* 610 (1968): 247.

53

natural history museum of fossils: Thomas Moynihan, *Spinal Catastrophism: A Secret History* (Falmouth: Urbanomic, 2019), 93–94.

glaciated temporality: Ibid., 89.

the wrecks of death are but a change of forms: Erasmus Darwin, *The Collected Writings of Erasmus Darwin* (London: Continuum, 2004), 161.

Some whorled shells have rolled out into the hall of minerals: "des coquillages ont roulé dans la salle des minéraux, et le nid d'un colibri repose sur la tête d'un crocodile." Qtd. in Walter Benjamin, *Das Passagen-Werk: Gesammelte Schriften,* ed. Rolf Tiedemann (Frankfurt-am-Main: Suhrkamp, 1982), I: 471/*The Arcades Project,* trans. Howard Eiland and Kevin McLaughlin (Cambridge: Harvard University Press, 1999), 377.

marble of its own tomb: "The marble mountain and the sparry steep/ Were built by myriad nations of the deep,—/ Age after age, who form'd their spiral shells…." Darwin, *The Collected Writings of Erasmus Darwin,* 161.

near Ise: Duncan Williams, *The Other Side of Zen: A Social History of Sōtō Zen Buddhism in Tokugawa Japan* (Princeton: Princeton University Press, 2009), 52.

54

In the blood pool: Ibid., 51.

The earth thickens with blood and waste: Robert Smithson, "The Artist and Politics: A Symposium," in *Robert Smithson: The Collected Writings,* ed. Flam, 135, 347, 100.

A point on a map expands: Robert Smithson, "Range of Convergence," in *Robert Smithson: The Collected Writings,* ed. Flam, 153.

55

The precious stones: "Oh les pierres précieuses qui se cachaient, — les fleurs qui regardaient déjà. [....] Oh les pierre précieuses qui s'enfouissant, et les fleurs ouvertes ! [....] et la Reine, la Sorcière qui allume sa brasie dans le pot de terre, ne voudra jamais nous raconter ce qu'elle sait, et que nous ignorons." Arthur Rimbaud, "Après le deluge," in *Complete Works: Selected Letters,* ed. Wallace Fowlie (Chicago: University of Chicago Press, 2005), 308.

56

archives of geology: Roger Caillois, *Pierres réfléchies* (Paris: Gallimard, 1975), 55.

Maya architecture: George Kubler, "The Design of Space in Mayan Architecture," and Mary Miller, "A Design for Meaning in Maya Architecture," in *Function and Meaning in Classic Maya Architecture,* ed. Stephen Houston (Dumbarton Oaks Research Library, 1998), 187.

58

gold and silver nuggets mined from Colombian canyons: Ricardo Becerra, "The Republic of Colombia," *Harper's New Monthly Magazine* 79, no. 474 (November 1889): 922.

gain in foreign trade for Great Britain: "Foreign Trade in 1900," *The Financial Review: Finance, Commerce, Railroads* (February 1901): 48.

annual world exportation of cotton: "Some Cotton Figures," *Scientific American Supplement,* no. 1522 (March 4, 1905): 24394.

the value of Indian rubber: "Trade with Other American Countries," *India Rubber Review,* June 15, 1915, 345.

the average export surplus of the United States: Federal Reserve Bank of New York, *Monthly Review of Credit and Business Conditions* (1945), 67.

the surplus just to Turkey: "Remarks of His Excellency Kenan Evren, President of the Republic of Turkey, at the Rayburn House Office Building, Washington. D.C., June 28, 1988," *Bulletin of the Assembly of Turkish American Associations* 9, no. 2 (1987–1988): 18.

capital outlays for resource development: *Public Papers of the Presidents of the United States: Harry S. Truman: 1946*, Vol. 2 (1962), 82.

retail and wholesale trade: California Franchise Tax Board, *Annual Report, Calendar Year 1961* (1962), 7.

Mexico's total monetary reserves: "The Economy," *Mexican-American Review* 39 (1971): 24.

the foreign exchange reserves held by Pakistan: "Editorial," *Pakistan and Gulf Economist* 4, no. 3 (1985): 8.

the cost of producing 416.5 million dollars: Jan ter Wengel, *Andean Market Allocation of Industry in the Andean Common Market* (The Hague: Martinus Nijhoff, 2012), 107.

Apache-basket: Lawrence Giffin, *Untitled, 2004: a poem* (New York: After Hours Editions, 2020), 39–40.

the same rate at which fertilizer was produced: *Summary of Findings and Recommendations* (Cleveland Department of Public Service), 142.

sundry unclassified minerals: New South Wales Department of Mines, *Annual Report for the Year 1907* (Sydney, 1908), 66.

59

toys, games, and sporting equipment: U.S. Department of Transportation, *Carload Waybill Statistics* (1990), 240.

Indian coal miners: *Records of the Geological Survey of India*, Vol. 86, Part II (1955), 337.

Glace Bay Public Building: *Sessional Papers* (Ontario, 1923), W-91.

the Mississippi below Davenport: *Iowa Legislative Documents*, Vol. 5 (1890), 830.

maximum grade: *Public Documents of Massachusetts* (1866), 42.
the San Joaquin & Tulare line: *The Railroad Gazette*, November 1, 1878, 447.
the Ohio Southern Railroad: *Annual Report of the Commissioner of Railroads and Telegraphs* (Ohio, 1888), 889.
the time it becomes necessary to stop and the time the vehicle begins to slow: George Lacy and Martin Barzelay, *Scientific Automobile Accident Reconstruction* (1898), 5–27; Anne Reynolds, *Robert Smithson: Learning from New Jersey and Elsewhere* (Cambridge: MIT Press, 2003), 180.
the starboard side of the Steamship Harvard: W.S. Leland and H.A. Everett, "Service Test of the Steamship Harvard," *International Marine Engineering* 13 (1908): 522.
the Chicago and Alton tracks: Missouri River Commission, *Descriptions and Elevations of Bench Marks on the Missouri River* (1912), 36.
Yerba Buena Mud: University of California, Berkeley, at Richmond, *Geotechnical Investigation Report: Northern Regional Library Facility Phase 4 Expansion* (2018), 11.
the Pont de Fleurs: Nathaniel Beardmore, *Manual of Hydrology* (London: Waterlow and Sons, 1872), 161.
the five-span bridge: Norfolk and Western Railway Company, unsigned notices, *Norfolk and Western Magazine* 42–43 (1964): 79.
pool stage of the Wylie Bridge: *Light List: Mississippi and Ohio Rivers and Tributaries, St. Louis District* (1942), 263.

61

potash, valued at $5.40: J.B. Lindsey, "Concerning Wheat Bran," *Hatch Experimental Station Public Document* 33 (January 1906): 113.
substandard levels of phosphorus: Morris Whitaker and Dale Colyer, *Agriculture and Economic Survival: The Role of Agriculture in Ecuador's Development* (Boulder: Westview Press, 1990), 150.

opium in Uttar Pradesh: Letizia Paoli, Victoria Greenfield, and Peter Reuter, *The World Heroin Market: Can Supply Be Cut?* (Oxford: Oxford University Press, 2009), 153.

the Canadian Border Patrol near Blaine: *United States–Canada Border Drug Threat Assessment* (October 2004).

per capita consumption of meat: Margaret Stella Chaney and Margaret Ahlborn, *Nutrition* (Boston: Houghton Mifflin, 1939), 370.

per capital consumption of beef: U.S. Department of Agriculture, *Foreign Agricultural Economic Report* (1974), 76.

Sotra brand Cold Smoked Salmon Fillets: FDA *Enforcement Report*, October 5, 1994.

feather and welter: Ashley Morrison, *The Professor: The Life Story of Azumah Nelson* (Houston: Strategic Book Publishing, 2014), 57; Deon Potgieter, *Rose of Soweto: The Dingaan Thobela Story* (Johannesburg: Penguin, 2012).

Billy Sherring: David Martin and Roger Gynn, *The Olympic Marathon: The History and Drama of Sport's Most Challenging Event* (Champaign: Human Kinetics, 2000), 61.

Ben Hogan: *World Book Encyclopedia*, Vol. 9: H (Chicago: World Book, 2007), 288.

measure of a talent: Marvin Sweeney, *I & II Kings: A Commentary* (Louisville: Westminster John Knox Press, 2013), 373.

Ohio Brass Company Porcelain Wall or Roof Insulator: Ohio Brass Company, *Catalog* 17 (Mansfield, 1919), 184.

Cammell & Co. compound armor plates: United States Board of Fortifications and Other Defenses, *Report Upon the Capacity of the Country to Furnish Armor and Guns* (Washington, DC: Government Printing Office, 1885), 17.

the average weight of an Amherst college student: E. Hitchcock, "Anthropometry," in *Proceedings of the American Association for the Advancement of Physical Education at Its Fifth Annual Meeting Held at Cambridge and Boston, Mass., April 4 and 5, 1890* (Ithaca: Andrus & Church, 1890), 7.

escape-and-evasion kit: Heritage Auctions, *Arms, Militaria, and Civil War Auction Catalog* 6050 (Dallas, 2010), item 52445.

Henry Sunde's Mexican San Jose de Agujas mine: *Mining World*, June 1, 1907, 709.

strong acid cationic exchanger: Canadian Mineral Processors, *Proceedings of the International Symposium on Gold (Winnipeg, Canada, August 23–26, 1987)* (Amsterdam: Elsevier, 1987), 367.

demolition of the Wharf mill: *U.S. Geological Survey Minerals Yearbook* (2004), 44.2.

Sultana claim: Geological Survey of Queensland, *Report* (1976), 113, 52.

63

"electrotype-therapeutic": Marco Fontani, *The Lost Elements: The Periodic Table's Shadow Side* (Oxford: Oxford University Press, 2014).

a limit for the leaching process: Shadia Ikhmayies et al., eds., *Characterization of Minerals, Metals, and Materials* (Hoboken: Wiley 2016), 340.

sulphite liquor: R.A. Strong, E. Swartzman and E.J. Burrough, *Fuel Briquetting*, Canada Bureau of Mines Reports, no. 775 (Ottawa: J.O. Patenaude, 1937), 89.

the new Kessler apparatus: Georg Lunge, *The Manufacture of Sulphuric Acid and Alkali with the Collateral Branches: A Theoretical and Practical Treatise* (New York: D. Van Nostrand, 1913), 1200.

cotton seeds: Mikhail Vladimirovich Gorlenko, *Bacterial Diseases of Plants* (Jerusalem: Israeli Program for Scientific Translations, 1965), 120.

Phaseolus groomed for starch formation: Wilrid Wyld, *Raw Materials for the Manufacture of Sulphuric Acid, and the Manufacture of Sulphur Dioxide* (New York: D. Van Nostrand, 1923), 18.

twenty tons of Russian lubricating oil: "Petroleum and Tar Oils Purified by a New Method," *Paint, Oil, and Drug Review* 24, no. 24 (December 15, 1897): 37.

the finest pitchblende: G.J. Rollandet, "Extraction of Radium Compounds from Ores: A Proposed Improvement Over the Methods of Curie and Debierne, as Indicated by a Recent Patent of Austrian Chemists: Description of Process," *Mining American* 64 (1912): 531.

nuclear plants with cation units: N.J. Ray, M. Ball, and D.J. Parry, "Condensate Purification Plant for Nuclear Systems," *Water Chemistry of Nuclear Reactor Systems* 2 (1981): 182.

Bulldog Mountain, north of Creede: Bureau of Mines, *Minerals Yearbook, Vol. II: Area Reports: Domestic* (Washington, DC: Government Printing Office, 1976), 160.

65

Is there measure on earth: Johann Christian Friedrich Hölderlin, "Giebt es auf Erden ein Maß? Es gibt keines," in *Sämtliche Werke: Briefe und Dokumente in zeitlicher Folge*, ed. D.E. Sattler, Bd. XII (Munich: Lucterhand, 2004), 23; qtd. in Franco "Bifo" Berardi, *Breathing: Chaos and Poetry* (South Pasadena: Semiotext(e), 2018), 19–20.

Measure is only a convention: Ibid., 19.

66

things exist: Stéphane Mallarmé, "Réponse à Jules Huret," in *Oeuvres complètes* (Paris: Gallimard, 2003), 871.

Every other science than Logic: Edgar Allan Poe, *Eureka: A Prose Poem* (Los Angeles; Green Integer, 2020), 74–75.

when one refuses to release scale from size: Smithson, "The Spiral Jetty," 147.

67

webs of manufactured time: Robert Smithson, "The Iconography of Desolation," in *Robert Smithson: The Collected Writings*, ed. Flam, 323.

lead and chromates from tire wear: Christian Neal MilNeil, "Inner-City Glaciers," in *Making the Geologic Now: Responses to Material Conditions of Contemporary Life*, eds.

Elizabeth Ellsworth and Jamie Kruse (Brooklyn: punctum books, 2013), 79.
a shadowy and fluctuating domain: Poe, *Eureka*, 30.
a beach made with dust: Paterson, *Ideas*.

68
Steno's Law: Moynihan, *Spinal Catastrophism*, 88.

71
Scale begins with the passional vortex: Charles Fourier, *Publication des manuscrits de Fourier*, Vol. IV, 1857–1858 (Paris: Librairie Phalanstérienne, 1858), 320.
A self-enclosed rotary of gyrating space: Smithson, "The Spiral Jetty," 146.
singularly the most abundant volcanic rock: Rayyane Tabet, "A Short History of Basalt," *Matthew Buckingham, Abraham Cruzvillegas, Mark Dion, Teresita Fernández, Trevor Paglen, Rayyane Tabet, Diana Thater on Robert Smithson*, eds. Katherine Atkins and Kelly Kivland (New York: Dia Art Foundatin, 2020), 150.
the questions mirrors ask: Robert Smithson, "Incidents of Mirror-Travel in the Yucatan," in *Robert Smithson: The Collected Writings*, ed. Flam, 124.
procession and cavalcade: "Fourier kennt viele Formen kollektiver Prozessionen und Aufzüge: orage, tourbillon, fourmilliere, serpentage [Fourier recognizes many forms of collective procession and cavalcade: storm, vortex, swarm, serpentage]." Benjamin, *Passagen-Werk*, 790/*Arcades Project*, 642.

72
Duration, since it is not absolute cannot be measured: Trevor Paglen, "Spiraling about Smithson," in *Matthew Buckingham, Abraham Cruzvillegas, Mark Dion, Teresita Fernández, Trevor Paglen, Rayyane Tabet, Diana Thater on Robert Smithson*, eds. Atkins and Kivland, 130.

73

an indexed codex such as a dictionary: C.T. Teng et al., US Patent No. 4,291,900 (September 29, 1981).

multiple signatures in a system: Post #14 in "Cosmic Signature Respawn," *Eve Forums*, https://forums-archive.eveonline.com/message/2420635/#post2420635.

74

hurricane of carnage: Robert Smithson, "Look," in *Robert Smithson: The Collected Writings*, ed. Flam, 370; perhaps from a conflation of the literal and social sense revolution, "hurricane," for Smithson, is a word associated with mass political violence: crusades which lead to the pursuit of multitudes, the destruction of civic space, war wounds, revolution against the war machine, etc. (ibid., 134, 308, 325, 370, *et passim*).

dissolving to a shapeless delirium: Smithson, "The Iconography of Desolation," 325.

75

lapidary mathematics: James Dwight Dana, *A System of Mineralogy: Including an Extended Treatise on Crystallography: with an Appendix, Containing the Application of Mathematics to Crystallographic Investigation, and a Mineralogical Bibliography* (New Haven: Durrie & Peck and Herrick & Noyes, 1837), 23–24.

fraught etymology: Jacob P. Dunn, "The Meaning of Tassinong," *Indiana Magazine of History* 11, no. 4 (December 1915): esp. 349.

76

Smithson saw the Guggenheim museum: Robert Smithson, "Quasi-Infinities and the Waning of Space," in *Robert Smithson: The Collected Writings*, ed. Flam, 35.

beautiful workshop gutter: F.T. Marinetti, "Manifeste de Futurisme," *Le Figaro*, February 20, 1909, 1.

77

"large spill" of crude oil: William Longley, Rodney Jackson, and Bruce Snyder, *Managing Oil and Gas Activities in Coastal Environments: Comprehensive Report* (Austin, 1982), 300.

Morgan Stanley: *Hearings Before the Permanent Subcommittee on Investigations of the Committee on Homeland Security and Governmental Affairs,* United States Senate, One Hundred Thirteenth Congress, Second Session, Vol. 1 (2014), 682.

per-household vehicle-fuel: *Household Vehicles Energy Consumption* (Department of Energy, 1993), 33.

Senate garage: "Report of the Secretary of the Senate," *Congressional Serial Set,* Vol. 9784 (73rd Congress, 2nd Session, 1933, Document No. 88), 281.

kerosene: *Annual Report of the Chief of Ordnance to the Secretary of War* (Washington, DC: Government Printing Office, 1892), 77.

Dungarvan: unsigned notice, *Chemical Trade Journal and Chemical Engineer* (1923): 579.

seal oil: Superintendent, Government Guano Islands Division, "Annual Report," *Commerce & Industry* 15 (1956): 300.

whale oil: Peter L. Payne, *Northern Scotland,* Vols. XVII–XVIII (Aberdeenshire: Centre for Scottish Studies 1997), 25.

78

cocoanut oil: *Report on the Administration of Port Blair of the Andaman and Nicobar Islands and the Penal Settlements of Port Blair and the Nicobars for the Year 1879–80* (Calcutta: Home, Revenue & Agricultural Department Press, 1880), 28.

16,627 seamen: *Report on Sanitary Measure in India in 1881–2,* Vol. XV (London: Eyre and Spottiswoode, 1883), 204.

"pure olive oil": "Pure Olive Oil," *Locomotive Fireman's Magazine* 25, no. 1 (July 1898): 154.

linseed oil: "Annual Report of the Canal Commissioners," *Documents of the Assembly of the State of New York,* Vol. 1, No. 9 (1866), 132.

winter oil: *Journal of the Select Council of the City of Philadelphia* (Philadelphia: Crissy & Markley, 1852), 84.
benzine: *Appendix to the Journals of the House of Representatives* [New Zealand] (1929), cvii.
turpentine gum: *Naval Stores Review & Terpene Chemicals* (New Orleans: H.L. Peace, 1971), 70.
copper preservative: *Report of the Director of Agriculture, British Guiana* (1958), 82.
bright varnish: *House Documents*, vol. IV, no. 174 (1862), 70.
Fluid Extracts and Tinctures: Department of Hospitals, *Annual Report* (New York: Hubner, 1930), 228.
creosote: "At the Inventions Exhibition," *The British Architect* (June 12, 1885): 282.

79

lasht: V. Lyavshuc, "Stephan Bathory and the Jesuits in Grodno," *Medieval and Early Modern Studies for Central and Eastern Europe* 2 (2010): 200.
Cornelius Quigg's still: "Frauds on the Internal Revenue," *House Documents* 3, no. 234 (Washington, DC: Government Printing Office, 1867), 184.
Marquis of Abercorn: John Gebbie, *An Introduction to the Abercorn Letters, as Relating to Ireland, 1736–1816* (Omagh: Strule Press, 1972), 183.
strong beer dispersed to the populace of Salisbury: Robert Moody, "James Bennet of Salisbury (1797–1859): Jeweller and Newspaper Proprietor," *The Wiltshire Archaeological & Natural History Magazine* 94 (2001): 184.
strong beer: *Sessional Papers of the Dominion of Canada*, Vol. 10, No. 15 (Ottawa, 1892), 67.
Cannington, Wapella, and Moosomin: David McGill, *The Guardians at the Gate: The History of the New Zealand Customs Department* (Wellington: Silver Owl Press, 1991), 55.
Wellington mercers: Barrie Trinder and Jeff Cox, *Yeoman and Colliers in Telford: Probate Inventories for Dawley, Lilleshall,*

Wellington and Wrockwardine 1660–1750 (Chichester: Phillimore, 1980), 332.

the poisoning arts: *Defoe's Review: Reproduced from the Original Editions* (New York: Columbia University Press, 1938), 310.

Red-Strakes and Golden Pippins: Charles Reginald Haines, *A Complete Memoir of Richard Haines (1633–1685): A Forgotten Sussex Worthy* (London: Harrison and Sons, 1899), 79.

whaling off Honfleur: J. Thierry du Pasquier, "The Whalers of Honfleur in the Seventeenth Century," *Arctic* 37 (1984): 533.

Kenilworth Castle: *Bradshaw's Descriptive Railway Hand-Book of Great Britain and Ireland,* Section III (1876), 19.

Verzenay, Ay, Cramant, and Avize: Thomas George Shaw, *Wine, the Vine, and the Cellar* (London: Longman, Green, Longman, Roberts, & Green, 1863), 225.

rain at Verzenay: *British Trade Journal* (January 1, 1884): 10.

Theobald le Botiller: *Her Majesty's Public Record Office, Calendar of Documents Relating to Ireland* (London: Longman & Co., 1877), 551.

Strobel and Church: *Tradesman, or Commercial Magazine: Including Subjects Relative to Commerce, Foreign and Domestic, together with Suggestions for New Commercial Connexions, Expositions of the History and Processes of Manufactories, &c.,* Vol. IV (London: Sherwood, Neely, & Jones, 1810), 184.

80

Pilgrims: Warren Sears Nickerson, *Land Ho! 1620*, ed. Dolores Bird Carpenter (East Lansing: Michigan State University Press, 1997), 16.

voyage aboard the Titanic: John P. Eaton and Charles A. Haas, *Titanic, Triumph and Tragedy,* 2nd edn. (New York: W.W. Norton, 1994), 336.

Portsmouth from Oporto on the Betty: Donald John MacLeod, *Hartleyana: Being Some Account of the Life and Opinions of Henry Robinson Hartley, Scholar, Naturalist, Eccentric and Founder of the University of Southampton* (Edinburgh: Scottish Academic Press, 1987), 25.

Sloop Betsey to the Sloop Liberty: *Virginia Magazine of History and Biography* (Richmond: Virginia Historical Society, 1980), 325.

the Lydia from the West Indies: William Threipland Baxter, *The House of Hancock: Business in Boston, 1724–775*, Vol. 10 (Cambridge: Harvard University Press, 1945), 125–26.

Christopher Leffingwell: *Dawson's Book Shop Catalogue* 180, item 232b (Los Angeles, privately printed), 27.

J. Cameron to G. Knight: W. Inglis, *Chambers's Educational Course: Book-keeping by Single and Double-entry: With an Appendix Containing Explanations of Mercantile Terms and Transactions* (Edinburgh: William and Robert Chambers, 1850), 125.

stevedores at Demerara: Robert White Stevens, *On the Stowage of Ships and Their Cargoes: With Information Regarding Freights, Charter-Parties, &c., &c.*, 7th edn. (London: Longmans, Green, And Co., 1894), 632.

the old Commissary department in Bethlehem: Richard K. Showman, ed., *The Papers of General Nathanael Greene*, Vol. 1: January 1777–16 October 1778 (Providence: Rhode Island Historical Society, 1976), 242.

intoxicating liquors: "City Marshal's Report," *Twelfth Annual Report of the Receipts and Expenditures of the City of Lewiston* [Maine] (1875), 97.

Hesperidina: *Great Britain House of Commons Sessional Papers: Inventory Control Record*, Vol. 92 (1905), 684.

expeditionary detachment of the Russian Army: C.E. Howard Vincent, *Russia's Advance Eastward* (London: Henry King, 1874), 27.

substandard alcohol: J.L. Black, *Russia and Eurasia Documents Annual*, Vol. 1 (Gulf Breeze: Academic International Press, 2008), 329.

apple brandy: Benjamin Vaughn Abbott, *A Digest of the Reports of the United States Courts*, Vol. IV (New York: Diossy and Company, 1885), 855.

Orme and Keigwin: "Commercial Causes," *The Magistrate* (July 2, 1906): 272.

Rhode and Thwaites: Alfred William Bays, *Cases on Commercial Law: General Survey, Contracts, Agency, Bailments, Sales, Negotiable Paper, Partnerships. Corporations, Bankruptcy*, 2nd edn. (Chicago: Callaghan and Co., 1923), 628.

Allen and Hodge: "Allen et al. v. Hodge (Court of Appeals of Kentucky, Dec. 18, 1907)," *The Southwestern Reporter* 106 (1908): 257.

Lambeth and Joffrion: "Lambeth v. Joffrion, Sheriff (Supreme Court of Louisiana, July Term, 1889)," *The Southern Reporter* 6 (1890): 559–60.

81

the most important plantation estate in Jamaica: *Accounts and Papers of the House of Commons*, Vol. XLVIII: Slavery (1836), 334.

Levy on the Florida peninsula: George Ripley and Charles Dana, eds., *The American Cyclopedia: A Popular Dictionary of General Knowledge*, Vol. X (New York: D. Appleton, 1875), 380.

U.S.S. Rattler: Charles W. Stewart, *Official Records of the Union and Confederate Navies in the War of the Rebellion*, Series I, Vol. 25 (Washington, DC: Government Printing Office, 1912), 271.

fraight in Hall: Warren Billings and Maria Kimberly, *The Papers of Sir William Berkeley: 1605–1677* (Richmond: Library of Virginia, 2007), 294.

adulterated "old tobacco": James Pagan, *Glasgow Past and Present*, Volume II (Glasgow: James Macnab, 1851), 122.

rotten on arrival: Patrick McGrath, *Merchants and Merchandise in Seventeenth-Century Bristol* (Bristol: Bristol Record Society, 1955), 253–54.

lodged without clearance: Edward Carson, *The Ancient and Rightful Customs: A History of the English Customs Service* (Hamden: Archon Books, 1972), 108.

John Fuller: *Sussex Archaeological Collections, Relating to the History & Antiquities of the County*, Vol. 104 (Sussex: Sussex Archaeological Society, 1966), 71.

the Success of Ayr: Eric Graham, *The Port of Ayr: 1727–1780* (Ayr: The Ayrshire Archaeological and Nautical Association, 1995), 16.

Sabine Hall: Louis Morton, "Robert Wormeley Carter of Sabine Hall: Notes on the Life of a Virginia Planter," *Journal of Southern History* 12 (1946): 362.

mean stuff: Winifred Proctor, "Poor Law Administration in Preston Union, 1838–1848," *Transactions of the Historic Society of Lancashire and Cheshire* 117 (1965): 146, 148.

Hamilton and Company: *Tradesman, or Commercial Magazine: Including Subjects Relative to Commerce, Foreign and Domestic, together with Suggestions for New Commercial Connexions, Expositions of the History and Processes of Manufactories, &c.*, Vol. IV (London: Sherwood, Neely, & Jones, 1810), 375.

Malta, via Rotterdam: Secretary of State, *Annual Report on Foreign Commerce*, Vol. 112 (Washington, DC: Government Printing Office, 1858), 20.

Leghorn: Secretary of State: *Annual Report on Commercial Relations* (Washington, DC: William Harris, 1874), 378.

Falls City steamer: Donald J. Wright, "Louisville Kentucky," *Waterways Journal* 64, no. 11 (March 10, 1951): 11

seven dollars and twenty cents: "Burley Tobacco Sells at Highest Prices in Years," *Wisconsin Equity News* 1, no. 16 (December 15, 1908): 16.

tobacco sales at Louisville: *The Commercial & Financial Chronicle, Bankers' Gazette, Commercial Times, Railway Monitor, and Insurance Journal* 4, no. 80 (1867): 861.

Internal Revenue seizure: John Melville Gould and George Fox Tucker, *Notes on the Revised Statues of the United States and Subsequent Legislation of Congress* (Boston: Little, Brown, & Co., 1889), 701.

freight rates from Paris to New Orleans: "Attacking Freight Rates on Tobacco," *United States Tobacco Journal,* November 16, 1912, 24.

82

a thirty-six foot car: George Wanless, "American Leaf Tobacco," *Bulletin of the American Warehousemen's Association* 22, no. 255 (May 1921): 177.

19,300,800 cigarettes: D.M. Wood et al., "'Pack Year' Smoking Histories: What About Patients Who Use Loose Tobacco?," *Tobacco Control* 14, no. 2 (April 2005): 141–42; John J. Scalon, "The Cigarette Craze," *The Lancet* (October 31, 1903): 126.

collapse of relative scales: Reynolds, *Robert Smithson,* 197.

powder cached: Evelyn Berckman, *Creators and Destroyers of the English Navy* (London: Hamish Hamilton, 1974), 187.

a Baiker in Perth: Thomas Laurence Kington-Oliphant, *The Jacobite Lairds of Gask* (London: Grampian Club, 1870), 165.

casks of loose skins: Walter E. Minchinton, "Richard Champion, Nicholas Pocock, and the Carolina Trade: A Note," *South Carolina Historical Magazine* 70–71 (1969): 99–100.

crystals, only as large as a pin point: F.S.S., sermon, *The Friend* (Honolulu: Hawaiian Evangelical Association, 1913), 252.

pease provisioned: Peter Goodwin, *Nelson's Ships: A History of the Vessels in Which He Served: 1771–1805* (London: Conway Maritime Press, 2002), 107.

herring: *Special Report on the Fisheries Protection Service of Canada, 1886–87* (1886), 33.

staves purchased from a cooper: John Sparrowhawk, "Divans and Cozy Corners," *The Ladies' Home Journal* 13 (1895), 17.

L'Aimable Henriette: T.S. Williams and Jules Lafont, *French and English Commercial Correspondence: A Collection of Modern Mercantile Letters in French and English with Their Translation on Opposite Pages,* 2nd edn. (London: Williams and Norgate, 1871), 193.

salt abated: *The Resources of the New England–New York Region* (Boston: New England–New York Inter-Agency Committee), 37.

83

a musket in the South China Sea: Daniel Henderson, *Yankee Ships in China Seas: Adventures of Pioneer Americans in the Troubled Far East* (New York: Hastings House, 1946), 106.

soup: Kenneth W. Milano, *History of the Kensington Soup Society* (Charleston: History Press, 2009), 153.

Israeli dairies: Esther Tauber, *Molding Society to Man: Israel's New Adventure in Co-operation* (New York: Bloch, 1955), 98; Shemu'el Dayan, *Man and the Soil: The History of the First Four Decades of Nahalal* (Tel-Aviv: Massadah, 1965), 108.

Aryshire-breed heifer: "2,800 Gns. Balig Heifer Establishes Two New Records," *The Ayrshire Cattle Society's Journal* 21 (1949): 305.

Dunlop Treasure: "Dunlop Place Annual Sale: Good Demand for Young Bulls," *Ayrshire Digest* 6 (1920): 18.

Mahananda cooperative: B.S. Baviskar and Donald W. Attwood, *Finding the Middle Path: The Political Economy of Cooperation in Rural India* (Oxford: Routledge, 2018).

pli selon pli: Stéphane Mallarmé, "à Ceux de l'Excelsior [now known as 'Remémoration d'amis belges']," *Magasin littéraire* 10, no. 2 (1893): 233.

guedoufle: *Larousse Universale,* 1922 and Randle Cotgrave, *Dictionarie of the French and English Tongues* (London: Adam Islip, 1632); on the word in Rabelais, see Michèle Schmidt-Küntzel's dissertation: *Cotgrave et sa source rabelaisinne: analyse synchronique et diachronique*, PhD Dissertation, University of Cologne, 1984, 126; see Michel Arrivé, *Les langages de Jarry: essai sémiotique littéraire* (Paris: Klincksieck, 1973), 211; Jarry uses the word in *L'amour absolu* (Paris: Mercure de France, 1952), 71; a possible corroboration comes from the Renaissance use of *gide* to signify "bas-ventre" in Nicolas de Cholières, *Les après disnées* (Paris: J. Richer, 1610).

84

gold dust and ivory: "Prize Courts Records," *Journal of the Barbados Museum and Historical Society* (1935): 189.

Peleg Green: The Massachusetts Historical Society, *Collections of the Massachusetts Historical Society,* Seventh Series, Volume IX (Boston, 1914), 378.

burnt in a Schooner: "The Marine List," *Lloyd's List* (rpt. Hants: Gregg International, 1969), 9.

shipped and received from Haiti to the United States: Robert Southey, "Works on England," *The Quarterly Review* 30 (1824): 573.

part maudite: Georges Bataille, *La part maudite* (Paris: Minuit, 1967).

what the despairing Sheriff made: *Reports of Cases Argued and Determined in the Supreme Court of Louisiana,* Vol. 41 (1889), 755.

Jamaica plantation: B.W. Higman, *Plantation Jamaica: 1750–1850* (Kingston: University of the West Indies Press, 2005), 261.

twelve aspents of Creole cane: "November Days From Old Plantation Diaries," *The Planter and Sugar Manufacturer* 21, no. 19 (November 5, 1898): 298.

bales of middling upland cotton: Edward Brooks, *Normal Higher Arithmetic Designed for Advanced Classes in Common Schools, Normal Schools, High Schools, Academies, etc.* (Philadelphia: Sower, Potts & Company, 1876), 94.

cold measure semi-sirup: H.W. Wiley, "Experiments with Sorghum Cane, 1883," *Report of the Commissioner of Agriculture* (47th Congress, 2nd Session, 1883, Executive Document No. 109), 429; *Experiments in Amber Cane and the Ensilage of Fodders at the Experimental Farm of the University of Wisconsin* (Madison: Democrat Printing, 1882), 59.

farmers of Liberty County: *Annual Report of the Agricultural Bureau* [Texas] (Austin, 1889), 139.

by the Philippine Islands: "The Sugar World," *The Beet Sugar Gazette* 6, no. 1 (1903): 76.

tricresol solution: P.L. Gile and C.N. Ageton, "The Red Clay Soils of Porto Rico," *Porto Rico Agricultural Experiment Station Bulletin*, No. 14 (Washington, DC: Government Printing Office, 1911), 18.
record-setting Seagrave: "Motor Fire Apparatus," *Fire and Water Engineering* 56, no. 1 (July 1, 1914): 29.
Allis-Chalmers Vertical Compound Engines: *Annual Report of the Water Commissioner* (St. Louis, 1917), 198.

85
irrigation per apple tree: "Deciduous Fruit Production," *International Encyclopaedia of Agricultural Science and Technology*, Vol. 2, eds. G. Sethuraman and Srinivasa Naidu (New Delhi: Mittal, 2008), 133.
condensed water: "The Cost of Condensing Water," *The Mechanical Engineer* 10, no. 3 (1885): 459.
amount wasted if a faucet runs: Nancy Miernickl, "Borough Authority Plans Survey for Water Leaks," *Republican and Herald*, Pottsville, PA, June 8, 1957, 42C.
Erie boiler: *Biennial Report of the State Board of Health of West Virginia* (Charleston: Cirque Printing, 1916), 243.
Number Sixteen Broad Street: unsigned notice, *New York Historical Society Journal* (1965): 184.
Doyle patented "fast-cycle": C.H. Vivian, "Cigarettes and Pneumatics," *Compressed Air Magazine* 72 (1967): 8.
Imhoff tank: *State Highway Commissioner to the Governor of Virginia*, Fourteenth Report (Richmond: Public Printing, 1921), 115.

86
South Weymouth, Massachusetts: M.M. Tidd, *Annual Report of the Water Commissioners* (1903), 267.
the steam engine at Doonan: William Wenman Seward, *Topographia Hibernica: Or the Topography of Ireland, Antient and Modern, giving a Complete View of the Civil and Ecclesiastical State of that Kingdom, with its Antiquities, Natural Curiosities, Trade, Manufactures, Extent and*

Population, The Whole Alphabetically Arranged (Dublin: Alex Stewart, 1795), s.v. "Maraghagh."

Mr. Blakey's patented steam engine: Graham Rees, ed., *The Cyclopædia, Or, Universal Dictionary of Arts, Sciences, and Literature*, Vol. XXXIV (London: Longman, Hurst, Rees, Orme, & Brown, 1819), s.v. "Steam-Engine."

Big Wood Ski Area: USDA *Forest Service, Draft Environmental Statement: Bigwood Ski Area* (Twin Falls: United States Department of Agriculture: Forest Service, 1974), 44.

Worthington compound duplex pump: *Annual Statistical Report of the Department of Health*, Vol. 34 (Albany: State Department of Health, 1914), 672.

the dump tank in Exeter: Royal Commission on Sewers, "Reports from Commissioners, Inspectors and Others," *Parliamentary Papers, House of Commons and Command*, Vol. 45: Sewage Disposal, continued (1908), 250.

Lancaster elementary school district: Los Angeles Board of Supervisors, *Statement of Bonded Indebtedness* (1941), 51.

youth population of Harlow: Youth Service Information Centre, *Year Book of the Youth Service in England & Wales* (London, 1971), 254.

Spanish Sahara: "Facts," *International Affairs* 6, pt. 2 (September 1960): 111.

Mahatpur, Nadiya: W.W. Hunter, *A Statistical Account of Bengal*, Vol. II (London: Trübner & Co., 1875), 136.

Peñaranda, Philippines: War Department, *Military Notes on The Philippines* (Washington, DC: Government Printing Office, 1898), 128.

Cattaro: *War Facts and Figures: An Encyclopedia of Useful Information with Maps and a Gazetteer* (London: British Dominions General Insurance Company, 1915), 171.

Dinuba: "Agriculture," *Community Service News*, September–October 1944, xiii.

Mola, Naples, or Giesse: *Edinburgh Gazetteer, or compendious Geographical Dictionary: Containing a Description of the Various Countries, Kingdoms, States, Cities, Towns, Mountains, Seas, Rivers, Harbours, &c. of The World; An*

Account of the Government, Customs, and Religion, of the Inhabitants; The Boundaries and Natural Productions of Each Country, &c. Forming a Complete Body of Geography, Physical, Political, Statistical, and Commercial, 2nd edn. (Edinburgh: Longman, Rees, Orme, Brown, and Green, 1829), 226.

the eight villages of Lathi, India: Loke Natha Ghose, *The Modern History of the Indian Chiefs, Rajas, Zamindars, &c., Part I: The Native States, comprising Geographical, Statistical, Historical, and Political Accounts of Every Native State in India* (Calcutta: Presidency Press, 1879), 162.

Marala, Pakistan: *Hand Book of Important Places in West Pakistan* (Lahore: Pakistan Social Service Foundation, 1965), 138.

87

Norman, Minnesota, or Santa Cruz: *Carroll's Municipal/County Directory* (Washington, DC: Carroll Publishing Co., 1999), 440; Sara Cameron and Ben Box, *Mexico and Central America Handbook* (Bath: Footprint, 1999), 682.

Privais: *Bradshaw's Illustrated Travellers' Hand-Book to France, adapted to all the railway routes: with a short itinerary of Corsica, and an introductory guide to Paris, with Maps, Town Plans, and Illustrations* (London: W.J. Adams, 1855), 149.

Bromberg, Prussia: Charles Saint-Laurent, *Dictionnaire Encyclopédique usuel, ou Résumé de tous les dictionnaires historiques, biographiques, géographiques, mythologiques, scientifiques, artistiques, technologiques, etc., présentant la définition exact et précise de 40,000 mots* (Paris: Guillaumin, 1862), 170.

Charlotte Amalie: *The Lincoln Library of Essential Information: An Up-to-Date Manual for Daily Reference, for Self-Instruction, and for General Culture* (Buffalo: Frontier Press, 1924), 674.

San Marino: A.J. du Pays, *Guide-Joanne: Itinéraire descriptif, historique, et artisitque de l'italie et de la sicile, quatrième édition, tome second: italie du sud* (Paris: Hachette, 1865), 11.

St. Helena: *Cambridge International Reference on Current Affairs, Atlas Pocket Guide to the World Today*, 5th edn. (London: DK, 2012), 364.

Sitka Borough: Dorothy Tegeler and Robin Nordhues, *Retiring in Arizona* (Baldwin Park: Gem Guides Book Company, 1994), 139.

Mojave County: Alfredo Gutierrez, "Foreword", in Philip R. Vandermeer, *Burton Barr: Political Leadership and the Transformation of Arizona* (Tucson: University of Arizona Press, 2014), x.

Jackson County: State Bank Commissioner, *Report* (Little Rock: State Bank Department, 1974), 157.

LaFayette County: A.W. Chase, *Dr. Chase's Home Adviser and Every Day Reference Book: A Companion to Dr. Chase's Receipt Books* (Detroit: F.B. Dickerson, 1894), 549.

Oregon City: William E. Powers and Richard F. Logan, eds., *Transcontinental Excursion Guidebook* (Washington, DC: International Geographical Union, 1952), 161.

Bend: unsigned tabulation, *Harmon Foundation Year Book* (New York: Harmon Foundation, 1926), 23.

Smiths Falls: *Industrial Water Resources of Canada: Water Survey Report* (1952), 86.

Corte Madera: *Roster: Federal, State, County, City, and Township Officials* (1966), 138.

Reykjavik: *Fodor's '98: Europe: The Best of 32 Countries with the Historic Towns, Great Cities, and Scenic Coasts and Countrysides* (New York: Fodor's, 1997), 558.

Sharkey County: D.L. Combs, R. Gibson Parrish, and Roy Ing, *Death Investigation in the United States and Canada* (Atlanta: Centers for Disease Control, 1990), 125 (other data from ibid., 127, 179, 111).

Makushi, Guyana: Janette Fort, *About Guyanese Amerindians* (Georgetown: Amerindian Research Unit, 1996), 15.

Schönheide, Erzgeb: "Cultivating Foreign Trade, Part IV," *Hardware Dealers' Magazine* 33, no. 5 (May 1910): 1141.

Gainesville, Texas: "Assessed Valuations and Tax Rates of Texas Cities," *The Bond Buyer* 55, no. 1413 (May 8, 1920): 9.

Lancaster, Pennsylvania: Edwin Williams, *A Comprehensive System of Modern Geography and History, Revised and Enlarged from the London Edition of Pinnock's Modern Geography, and Adapted to the Use of Academies and Schools in the United States* (New York: Bliss, Wadsworth & Co., 1835), 126.

Wagga Wagga: United States Department of Commerce, *Commercial Travelers' Guide to the Far East,* Trade Promotion Series No. 29 (Washington, DC: Government Printing Office), 329.

Dickenson Virginia: Henry Gannett, *A Gazetteer of Virginia* (Washington, DC: Government Printing Office, 1904), 50.

Fostoria, Ohio: *Ohio: Federal, State, County, Township and Municipal Officers* (Springfield: Springfield Publishing, 1907), 346.

Tucker County: Bureau for Government Research, *The West Virginia Political Almanac* (West Virginia University, 1964), 168.

Plainfield, New Hampshire: *New Hampshire Register, State Yearbook and Legislative Manual,* Issue 213 (Standish: Tower Publishing, 2014), 583.

island of Ofu: Arthur Dahl, *Island Directory* (Gland: United Nations Environmental Programme, 1991), 405.

non-indigenous population in Indonesia: W.M.F. Mansvelt et al., *Changing Economy in Indonesia,* Vol. 11: *Population Trends: 1795–1942* (Amsterdam: Royal Tropical Institute, 1991), 99.

white population in Harlem: Department of Health, City of New York, *Fourth Annual Report of the Woman's Auxiliary to the New York Department of Health Tuberculosis Clinics,* Monograph Series No. 10 (December, 1913), 27.

men in Karabük: Arama Sonuçları, "Geographical Distribution of the Consumption of Alcoholic Beverages in Turkey," in *İstanbul Üniversitesi Coğrafya Enstitüsü* (Istanbul: IU Press, 1951), 256.

Catholics in Katunayake: J.B. Clinton Anandappa, *The Catholic Directory of Sri Lanka, 1989/90* (Ragama: self-published, 1990), 171.

deaf population of New Zealand: David McKee, Rachel McKee, and George Major, "Numerical Variation in New Zealand Sign Language," *Sign Language Studies* 12, no. 1 (Fall 2011): 72–97.

88

Continental Army: Ricardo Herrera, *For Liberty and the Republic: The American Citizen as Soldier, 1775–1861* (New York: NYU Press, 2015), 31.

rocky fastness: Manuel Márquez-Sterling, *Fernán González, First Count of Castile: The Man and the Legend* (Oxford: Romance Monographs, 1980), 9.

Route Ten: *Bradshaw's Illustrated Hand-Book to Switzerland the Tyrol; with Maps and Engravings*, new edn. (Manchester: Henry Blacklock, 1857), 62.

Calgiari sheep: Patrick F. Fox and Paul L.H. McSweeney, *Encyclopedia of Dairy Sciences* (Amsterdam: Elsevier, 2011).

hectare of fava beans: R.J. Summerfield, ed.,*World Crops: Cool Season Food Legumes: A Global Perspective of the Problems and Prospects for Crop Improvement in Pea, Lentil, Faba Bean and Chickpea* (New York: Springer 2012), 1147.

corn residue: O.C. Sitton et al., "Ethanol Production from Agricultural Residues," in *Encyclopedia of Chemical Processing and Design*, eds. Willaim A. Cunningham and John J. McKetta, Jr. (London: Taylor & Francis, 1976), 40.

89

lynxes: Isidore of Seville, *Etymologies*, XII, 2.20.

cadena perpetua: War Department, *Translation of the Penal Code in Force in The Philippines* (Washington, DC: Government Printing Office, 1900), 142.

trachea, bronchia, et seq.: Samuel Wright, "Pathology of Expectoration," *The Medical Times* 11, no. 272 (December 7, 1844): 200.

90

Blue Whale: Dan Bortolotti, *Wild Blue: A Natural History of the World's Largest Animal* (New York: St. Martin's Press, 2008), 250.

arable hectare: Frederick Wells, *The Long-Run Availability of Phosphorus: A Case Study in Mineral Resource Analysis* (Baltimore: Johns Hopkins University Press, 1975), 37–38, 44.

rotation of winter-cover crops: John S. Steinhart and Carol E. Steinhart, "Energy Use in the U.S. Food System," *Science* 184, no. 4134 (April 14, 1974): 307–16.

acre of wheat: Faculty of Agriculture, *Food Production and Consumption in Pakistan* (Lyallpur: West Pakistan Agricultural University Press, 1967), 55.

one thousand bricks: "Ceramic Abstracts 14," *Journal of the American Ceramic Society* 17 (1934): 128.

one hundred pounds of dried hay feed: *Encyclopedia Americana: A Library of Universal Knowledge*, Vol. X (New York: Encyclopedia Americana Corporation, 1918), 105.

one hundred bushels: "Flour and Grist-Mill Data — Sheet No. 1," *Electrical Review and Western Electrician* 62, no. 22 (1913): 1172.

electric oven: Jeffrey Langholz and Kelly Turner, *You Can Prevent Global Warming* (Kansas City: Andrews McMeel, 2003), 53.

increase of residential consumer: *Byllesby Management* 7 (1932): 13.

frozen-food-locker: S.T. Warrington, *Operation of Cooperative Frozen Food Locker Plants in Illinois: An Analysis of Investment, Operating Cost, and Income* (Washington, DC: Farm Credit Administration, 1941), iv.

Sunset line: "Report of One-Man Car Operation," *AERA* 7, no. 1 (August 1918): 39.

elevator running at full speed: William S. Monroe, "Tests of Electric Elevators," *The Engineering Record* 38, no. 18 (October 1, 1898): 385.

acre-foot: Hy Almond and Harold Bloom, *A Semimicro Method for the Determination of Cobalt in Soils and Rocks: A Field Test Using the Chromograph,* U.S. Geological Survey Circular 125 (October, 1951), 29.
reign of gallant Menes: John Eadie, *Early Oriental History: Comprising the Histories of Egypt, Assyria, Persia, Lydia, Phrygia, and Phoenicia* (London: John Joseph Griffin, 1852), 52; Josiah Conder, *The Modern Traveller,* Vol. XVII: Arabia (London: Thomas Tegg & Son, 1825), 60.
Arabia Petraea: Walter Chamberlain, *A Plain Reply to Bishop Colenseo, Respectfully Addressed to the Laymen of England* (London: Wertheim, Macintosh, and Hunt, 1863), 179.

91
biomass compacted: Bataille, *La part maudite.*

92
A lintie chittles: "The Bridegroom Darg," in *Remains of Nithsdale and Galloway Song: with Historical and Traditional Notices Relative to the Manners and Customs of the Peasantry,* ed. R.H. Cromek (London: Cadell and Davies, 1810), 119.
The frond uncoils, the bindweed shrinks: Waldo Dunn, *D. Blackmore: The Author of Lorna Doone* (Berkeley: University of California Press, 1956), 61.

93
Fern seed congeals: James George Frazer, *The Golden Bough: A Study in Magic and Religion,* Vol. 3, 2nd edn. (London: MacMillan, 1900), 341–55.
scattered among wilted fern and rose: Charles Baudelaire, "Spleen [II]," in *Les fleurs du mal,* trans. Anthony Hecht, *Baudelaire in English,* eds. Carol Clark and Robert Sykes (London: Penguin, 1997), 91.
Degrees of petiolation divide the tribes: Robin Joyn Tillyard, *The Biology of Dragonflies: Odonata or Paraneuroptera* (Cambridge: Cambridge University Press, 1917), 64.

95

indifferent to action: Robert Vilain, "Jugendstil," in *Encyclopedia of German Literature,* ed. Matthias Konzett (Chicago: Fitzroy Dearborn, 2000), 545.

never-ending curve: "la même délectation placée dans la courbe qui n'en finit plus comme celle de la fougère naissante, de l'ammonite ou de l'enroulement embryonnaire [the same delight in infinite curves like those of a budding fern, ammonite, or curled fetus]." André Breton, *Point du jour* (Paris: Imprimerie Crété, 1934), 234.

96

ancient fluted columns of horsetails: Walter Benjamin, "Kleine Geschichte der Photographie," in *Gesammelte Schriften,* eds. Rolf Tiedemann and Hermann Schweppenhauder (Frankfurt am Main: Suhrkamp Verlag, 1977), 2:371; trans. Phil Patton as "A Short History of Photography," *Artforum* 15, no. 6 (February 1977): 51.

pathos of form: Christoph Schreier, "Nature As Art — Art As Nature," in *Karl Blossfeldt: Photography* (Ostfildern: Cantz, 1994).

the two poles of past and future: Karl Nierendorf, *Art Forms in Nature* (New York: Weyhe, 1935), iii.

101

John Frémont: William L. Fox, *The Void, The Grid & The Sign: Traversing the Great Basin* (Reno: University of Nevada Press, 2016).

more desert than the sands that surrounded it: Dale Morgan, *The Great Salt Lake* (Indianapolis: Bobbs-Merrill, 1947).

Kate Conner: David E. Miller, "Great Salt Lake and Its Islands," in *Great Salt Lake National Park in Utah* (Washington, DC: U.S. Government Printing Office, 1961), 160.

102

Petroglyph spirals: Steven J. Manning, "The Fugitive-Pigment Anthropomorphs of Eastern Utah: A Shared Cultural Trait

Indicating a Temporal Relationship," *Utah Rock Art* 23 (2003): 110.

dark arching caverns: Homer, *Odyssey,* trans. Emily Wilson (New York: Norton, 2017), Book IX.

bare edge a watery abyss: Paul the Deacon, *History of the Lombards,* trans. William Didley Foulke, ed. Edward Peters (Philadelphia: University of Pennsylvania Press, 2003), 9–10.

103

The inorganic world could: Loren Eisley, *The Firmament of Time* (New York: MacMillan, 1960), 122.

tell the names of pain: Homer, *Odyssey,* Book XII.

speak to the shore: "Fractasque a litore voces." Virgil, *Aeneid* 9: 503.

the whirlpool can be conquered: Eisley, *The Firmament of Time,* 146.

104

hog-chain: Peter G. Van Alfen, "Sail and Steam: Great Salt Lake's Boats and Boatbuilders, 1847–1901," *Utah Historical Quarterly* 63, no. 3 (Summer 1995): 201.

105

extreme distress: J.A. Simpson and E.S.C. Weiner, eds., *The Oxford English Dictionary,* 2nd edn. (Oxford: Clarendon Press, 1989), s.v. "S.O.S."

pride and joy: Annie Call Carr, ed., for The Daughters of Utah Pioneers, *East of Antelope Island* (Kaysville: Davis County Company, 1948), 29.

consequence: Solomon F. Kimball, "Early-Day Recollections of Antelope Island," *Improvement Era* 10, no. 5 (March 1907): 336.

Salicornia: Stansbury, *An Expedition to the Valley of the Great Salt Lake of Utah,* 11; Stansbury overstates the class considerably; a more modest yawl or dorie would have been more accurate (Gary Topping, *Great Salt Lake: An Anthology* [Logan: Utah State University Press, 2002], 224).

frigate et seq.: Stansbury, *An Expedition to the Valley of the Great Salt Lake of Utah*, 11.

Black Rock: "Low Water of Great Salt Lake Reveals Ghosts of the Past," *Salt Lake Tribune*, August 18, 2014.

submerged the spit: Topping, *Great Salt Lake*, 208; Marlin Stum, *Visions of Antelope Island and Great Salt Lake* (Logan: Utah State University Press, 1999), 125.

106

spears: Brian Mullahy, "Great Salt Lake Gives Up 'Mysteries' as Water Drops," KUTV, November 5, 2014.

sailing cloth, et seq.: President Young's journal of 30 January, 1854: "I christened her the Timely Gull. She is forty-five feet long and designed for a stern wheel to be propelled by horses working a treadmill, and to be used mainly to transport stock between the city and Antelope Island." Other accounts describe the gull "fitted-up as a sailing boat." *Journal History of the Church*, June 25, 1856, LDS Archives; see also Stum, *Visions of Antelope Island and Great Salt Lake*, 127.

flagstone, cedarwood and salt: Andrew Jensen, *Latter-Day Saint Biographical Encyclopedia: A Compilation of Biographical Sketches of Prominent Men and Women in the Church of Jesus Christ of Latter-day Saints,* Vol. II (Salt Lake City: Andrew Jensen History Company, 1920), 660; David E. Miller, "Great Salt Lake: A Historical Sketch," *Utah Geological and Mineral Society Bulletin* 116 (June 1980): 12.

Lake isles: Bill Durham, "Sailors of the Briny Shallows," *Westways* 49 (Los Angeles: Automobile Club of Southern California, March, 1957), 52.

attack: Thomas G. Alexander, *Brigham Young and the Expansion of the Mormon Faith* (Norman: University of Oklahoma Press, 2019), 292; Richard Tomas Ackley, "Across the Plains in 1858," *Utah Historical Quarterly* 9 (1941): 190–218; Peter Gottfredson, ed., *History of Indian Depredations in Utah* (Salt Lake City: Skelton, 1919), *passim.*

scrap-iron: Topping, *Great Salt Lake*, 205.

107

scroll finial: Ephraim Segerman, "The Sizes of English Viols and Talbot's Measurements," *Galpin Society Journal* 48 (March 1995): 33–45.

prodigious specimen: Edward Boden, ed., *Black's Veterinary Dictionary*, 19th edn. (Lanham: Barnes & Noble, 1998), 282.

collagen: Voichita Bucur, *Handbook of Materials for String Musical Instruments* (Switzerland: Springer, 2016), 482–86.

potash: Bettina Hoffman, *The Viola de Gamba*, trans. Paul Ferguson (London: Routledge, 2018), 43.

amber: Ibid., 45.

lowest: Atthanasio Kircher, *Musurgia universalis sive ars magna consoni et dissoni in X. libros digesta*, Lib. V (Rome: Corbelletti, 1650), 440.

184,320: Sadly, this is almost sixty-five times the heads available to Young from his historic herd and two orders of magnitude larger than the common Church holdings at the time.

baroque-era pitch: Bruce Haynes, *A History of Performing Pitch: The Story of "A"* (Oxford: Scarecrow, 2002).

tension: the absolute mensur of a D string, in actuality, cannot practically exceed 79 cm given that its breaking point is a tone lower at 88.7 cm, calculated from the limit of approximately 260Hz per metre, a value independent of diameter. See Hoffmann, *The Viola de Gamba*, 41.

fatal winter: William Mulder, review of Norman F. Furniss, *The Mormon Conflict: 1850–1859* (New Haven: Yale University Press, 1960), *History News* 16, no. 12 (November 1960–October 1961): 145.

108

groove: Alexis Madrigal, "The Music Is Waiting to be Tapped: Listening in the Era of the Stream," *The Atlantic*, August 9, 2013, https://www.theatlantic.com/technology/archive/2013/08/the-music-is-waiting-to-be-tapped-listening-in-the-era-of-the-stream/278466/; Robert Harley,

"An LP Primer: How the LP Works," *The Absolute Sound* (June/July 2007): 36.

mirror surfaces disconnected: Smithson, "Incidents," in *Robert Smithson: The Collected Writings*, ed. Flam, 128 *et passim.*

109

rotating space station: Angeli Bukley and Gilles Clément, eds., *Artificial Gravity* (New York: Springer, 2007), 47.

Eifel field: Michael Weber et al., "Upper Mantle Structure Beneath the Eifel from Receiver Functions," in *Mantle Plumes: A Multidisciplinary Approach,* eds. Joachim R.R. Ritter and Ulrich R. Christensen (Berlin: Springer, 2007).

Wollops Island: Arthur J. Kantor and Allen E. Cole, *Monthly Midlatitude Atmospheres, Surface to 90 km* (Hanscom: Air Force Geophysics Laboratory, 1976), 16.

Dactyl satellite: Evgenii Mikhailovich Levin, *Dynamic Analysis of Space Tether Missions* (San Diego: American Astronautical Society), 22.

Acritarchs: Andrew Y. Glikson, *The Asteroid Impact Connection of Planetary Evolution* (Berlin: Springer, 2013), 107.

Chesapeake impact structure: Alessandro Montanari and Christian Koeberl, *Impact Stratigraphy: The Italian Record* (Berlin: Springer, 2006), 132.

Mammoth Wash: William Dickinson, *Kinematics of Transrotational Tectonism in the California Transverse Ranges and Its Contribution to Cumulative Slip Along the San Andreas Transform Fault System* (Boulder: Geological Society of America, 1996), 9–10.

Tanimbar Islands: Tomas Tomascik and Anmarie Mah, *Ecology of the Indonesian Seas* (Jakarta: Tuttle, 2013), fig. 4.14.

Twin Otter: Minerals Management Service, *Alaska Outer Continental Shelf Region, Proposed Diapir Field Lease Offering* (Washington, DC: Department of the Interior, 1984), 89.

Alfred Leblanc: S.N.D. North, ed., *The American Yearbook: A Record of Events and Progress* (New York: D. Appleton and Company, 1911), 710.

110

William Odom: Hanry Holden, *Teterboro Airport* (Charleston: Arcadia, 2010).

Council Bluffs: *The Tribune Almanac,* ed. Henry Eckford Rhoades (1899): 212–13.

D-Züge Reichsbahn express: Alfred Mierzejewski, *The Most Valuable Asset of the Reich: A History of the German National Railway, Volume 1, 1920–1932* (Chapel Hill: University of North Carolina Press, 2014), 42.

27-horsepower Pathfinder: "English High-Gear Tests: Royal Automobile Club Tries Out Pathfinder on 1,934.75-Mile Run with High Gear Continually in Mesh," *The Automobile* (October 24, 1912): 847.

American car on the banked circuit at Brooklands: "Motoring," *The Academy and Literature* 83 (1912): 491.

Marcel Duchamp: "C'est fini, la peinture. Qui ferait mieux que cette hélice," qtd. in *Etant donné* 1 (1999): 134. On Duchamp and spirals more generally, see Israel, *Spirals,* 111–139.

Filippo Tommaso Marinetti: "une automobile rugissante, qui a l'air de courir sur de la mitraille, est plus belle que la Victoire de Samothrace." Marinetti, "Manifeste," 1. On spirals in Italian Futurism generally, see Israel, *Spirals,* 49–59.

111

Estrada de Ferro São Eduardo: "Brazil: Railway Mileage and Construction," *Monthly Bulletin* (Washington, DC: Bureau of American Republics, 1898), 1463.

El Prado: "Steam Railroads," *Poor's Manual of Railroads* 53 (1920): 1210; John Moody, *Moody's Analyses of Investments: Part I — Steam Railroads* (New York: Moody's Investment Service, 1919), 885.

Hornos line: *Railway Age*, March 18, 1904, 479.

Marquette and Southeastern Rail Road: unsigned tabulation, *Poor's Manual of Railroads* (New York: Poor's Manual Company, 1917), 867.

average mileage run per drive per day: *Votes and Proceedings of the Legislative Assembly* (Victoria, 1928), 43.

Typiza: *Intercontinental Railway Commission, Condensed Report,* Vol. I, Part I (Washington, DC: IRC, 1898), 142.

Yanacancha: Herman G. Brock, *Markets for Boots and Shoes in Chile and Bolivia* (Washington, DC: Government Printing Office, 1918), 128.

Toyota iQ microcar: Engelbert Wimmer, *Motoring the Future: VW and Toyota Vying for Pole Position* (New York: Palgrave, 2011).

Upper Charley: USDA Forest Service, Pacific Northwest Region, *Draft Environmental Impact Statement* (April 2000), III:20.

belt of lignite: Brock, *Markets for Boots and Shoes in Chile and Bolivia,* 23.

Ma'sal of Haliban: Scott Fitzgerald Johnson, ed., *Oxford Handbook of Late Antiquity* (Oxford: Oxford University Press, 2012).

Bandar Shapur: Eleanor H. Tejirian and Reeva Spector Simon, *The Creation of Iraq, 1914–1921* (New York: Columbia University Press, 2004).

Qatar Peninsula: Lisa McCoy, *Qatar* (Broomall: Mason Crest, 2014).

Golan Heights: Michael Goodspeed, *When Reason Fails: Portraits of Armies at War: America, Britain, Israel, and the Future* (Westport: Praeger, 2002), 112.

Lebanon: Lamia Rustum Shehadeh, "Impact of Armed Conflict on Gender Roles in Lebanon," in *Gender and Violence in the Middle East,* eds. Fatima Sadiqi and Moha Ennaji (London: Taylor & Francis, 2011), Chapter 5.

Babylon: Donald Longmead and Christine Garnaut, *Encyclopedia of Architectural and Engineering Feats* (Santa Barbara: ABC-CLIO, 2011), 27.

Yongbyon: Andrei Lankov, *The Real North Korea: Life and Politics in the Failed Stalinist Utopia* (Oxford: Oxford University Press, 2013).

Lake Naivasha: Bram Büscher and Veronica Davidov, *The Ecotourism-Extraction Nexus: Political Economies and Rural*

Realities of (un)Comfortable Bedfellows (London: Taylor & Francis, 2013), 56.

Jinja: Richard Heinzl, *Cambodia Calling: A Memoir from the Frontlines of Humanitarian Aid* (Mississauga: Wiley, 2009).

Ayutthaya: B. Burnett Brown, *Thailand Destinations: Tips, Insights and Helpful Information* (n.p.: Xlibris, 2013).

Cambridge: 李学萍 et al., 大学英四考最新真解析: 全真模解析 (Tsinghua: 大学出版社, 2005), 317.

Haida Gwaii: G. Carleton Ray and Jerry McCormick-Ray, *Marine Conservation: Science, Policy, and Management* (Oxford: Wiley, 2013), 265.

Western Ghats: Francis Ching et al., *A Global History of Architecture* (Oxford: Wiley, 2011), 181.

112

El Brezo: William Christian, *Person and God in a Spanish Valley*, rev. edn. (Princeton: Princeton University Press, 1989), 54–55.

Limburg to Antwerp: Morris F. La Croix and Alfred H. Brooks, *The Iron and Associated Industries of Lorraine, the Saare District, Luxemburg, and Belgium* (Washington, DC: Department of the Interior, 1920), 88.

the strike of the Idaho rift: Jack Green and Nicholas Martin Short, *Volcanic Landforms and Surface Features: A Photographic Atlas and Glossary* (Berlin: Heidelberg, 2012), pl. 83A.

Cajon Pass: Rose Blue and Corinne Naden, *Exploring the Western Mountains* (Chicago: Raintree, 2004), 36.

Jellinbah open pit mine: *Minerals Yearbook: Area Reports: International: Asia and the Pacific* (Washington, DC: Department of the Interior, 2007), 19, 22, 24.

Attawapiskat: *Minerals Yearbook Area Reports: International Review: Latin America and Canada* (Washington: Geologic Survey, 2011), 5–12, 5–18.

Niamey: *Minerals Yearbook Area Reports: International Africa and the Middle East*, Vol. III (Washington: Geologic Survey, 2007), 26–11.

Tha Luang: Bureau of Mines, *Minerals Yearbook* 3, no. 3 (1996): 859, 966.
Ruta Nacional 40: Lorraine Caputo, *V!va Travel Guides Argentina* (Quito: Viva Publishing, 2011).
Moalboal: Dominique Grele and Lily Yoursy-Jouve, *100 Resorts in the Philippines: Places with a Heart* (Mandaluyong City: Asiatype, 2004), 204.
observing facilities on Kitt Peak: "Kitt Peak National Observatory," *Reporter* 31 (1984): 7.
Kyushu: James Lewis, *Frontier Contact Between Choson Korea and Tokugawa Japan* (London: Taylor & Francis, 2005), 17.
Sahul: Brian Fagan, *Beyond the Blue Horizon: How the Earliest Mariners Unlocked the Secrets of the Oceans* (New York: Bloomsbury, 2012), 35.
cross-country ski trails: Emmannuelle Alspaugh, *Norway*, 8th edn. (New York: Fodor's Travel Publications, 2006), 46.
Dr. Awótáyọ̀'s hospital: Mary Adekson, *The Yoruba Traditional Healers of Nigeria* (London: Taylor & Francis, 2004).
the Stillwater Range: Jose Collazo, *God Does Exist No More Nuclear Testing and More* (n.p.: Xlibris, 2012), 22.
the span of the Baetis: Brian Campbell, *Rivers and the Power of Ancient Rome* (Chapel Hill: University of North Carolina Press, 2012), 249.
Mandalay to the Kinda Irrigation Scheme: Edward Rice, *Paddy Irrigation and Water Management in Southeast Asia* (Washington: World Bank, 1997), 30.
the sewer system in Lima: Brock, *Markets for Boots and Shoes in Chile and Bolivia*, 137.

113

the water supply system of Shamokin: unsigned tabulation, *Insurance Yearbook* (New York: Spectator, 1912), C-435.
Bering Strait: Gina Misiroglu, *Handy Answer Book for Kids (and Parents)* (Canton: Visible Ink Press, 2009), 22.
the mainland oscillates: Smithson, "The Spiral Jetty," 146.

114

The shore of the lake became the edge of the sun: Ibid.

chaos of cracks: Robert Smithson, "Crystal Land," in *Robert Smithson: The Collected Writings*, ed. Flam, 9.

An infinity of surfaces: Smithson, "Entropy and the New Monuments," 11.

115

petrified birds: Rosemary Gudmundson Palmer, *Jim Bridger: Trapper, Trader, and Guide* (Minneapolis: Compass Point Books, 2007), 41.

Laguna de los Timpanogos: Raye Carleson Ringholz, *Barrier of Salt: The Story of Great Salt Lake* (Salt Lake City: Deseret Book Company, 1970), 20.

116

the first glume: Albert Radford et al., *Manual of the Vascular Flora of the Carolinas* (Chapel Hill: University of North Carolina Press, 2010), 75.

glabrous, slender, distending stem: Bernard Verdcourt, *Flora of Tropical East Africa: Moringaceae* (London: Taylor & Francis, 1986), 6.

coriaceous and strongly involute lemmas: E.H. Moss and John G. Packer, *Flora of Alberta* (Toronto: University of Toronto Press, 1983), 49, 103, 110, 142, 548, 579, 125.

fimbriate or sometimes shortly dentate: Berndt and Elizabeth George, *Verticordia* (Camberra: University of Western Australia Press, 2002), 94–96, 336, 354.

Solanum salasianum: Carlos Ochoa, *The Potatoes of South America: Peru, Wild Species*, Part 1 (Lima: International Potato Center, 2004), 207.

narrowly ovate spathes: *Flora of Tropical East Africa: Hydrocharitaceae* (London: Royal Botanical Gardens, 1989), 3.

narrowly lanceolate lamina: A. Lowrie and S. Carlquist, "Drosera silvicola," *Phytologia* 73, no. 2 (1992): 236.

spikelets and awns: Ronald Jones, *Plant Life of Kentucky* (Lexington: University Press of Kentucky, 2005).

loosely clustered sporocarps: H.J. Beentje, S.A. Ghazanfar, and R.M. Polhill, *Flora of Tropical East Africa* (London: Royal Botanical Gardens, 2003), 3, 10, 14.

scarce purple and gold: Chris Manley, *British Moths,* 2nd edn. (London: Bloomsbury, 2015), 18, 86, 106, 108, 110.

117

strongly granulose: S.E. Crumb, "Tobacco Cutworms," *Department of Agriculture Technical Bulletin* 88 (1929): 125.

anastrepha fruit fly: A. Stone, "The Fruit Flies of the Genus Anastrepha," *Department of Agriculture Miscellaneous Publication* (1942): 27.

effective evapotranspiration: A.J. Thomas et al., *Land Use Changes in Europe Processes of Change, Environmental Transformations and Future Patterns* (Amsterdam: Springer, 2012), 285.

bands used to track common bird species: Parque Etnobotánico Omora, *Magellanic Sub-Antarctic Ornithology: First Decade of Long-term Bird Studies at the Omora Ethnobotanical Park, Cape Horn Biosphere Reserve, Chile* (Denton: University of North Texas Press, 2014), 120.

omnidirectional passive barrier trap: Richard Smitz, *A Passive Aerial Barrier Trap Suitable for Sampling Flying Bark Beetles* (Champaign: University of Illinois Press, 2010), 3.

the white stripe: Federal Register, *The Code of Federal Regulations of the United States of America* (Washington, DC, 1980), 297.

granular rubber shreds: Rafat Siddique, *Waste Materials and By-Products in Concrete* (Berlin: Springer, 2007), 135.

vertable screw rod: Edward Benzel, *Spine Surgery* 2 (Philadelphia: Elsevier, 2012), 1348.

medullary canal: David Stanley and Ian Trail, *Operative Elbow Surgery* (Edinburgh: Elsevier, 2011), 330, 394.

end-diastolic wall: Ernst van der Wall et al., *Myocardial Viability* (Amsterdam: Springer, 2012), 187.

118

preoperative pupil size: Christopher Rapuano, *Year Book of Ophthalmology* (Philadelphia: Elsevier, 2012), 48.

medial rectus: Al Lens et al., *Ocular Anatomy and Physiology* (Thorofare: slack, 2008), 39.

the base of the perianth: Sarah Smith and Jonathan Stansbie, *Flora of Tropical East Africa: Alliaceae* (London: Taylor & Francis, 2003), 5.

the ampulla to the posterior semicircular canals: William Pellet et al., *Otoneurosurgery* (Berlin: Springer, 2012), 31.

119

lecture and practical work requirements: Jean Leclercq, *How to Qualify as a "Biologist" in the Universities of Europe* (Strasbourg: Council for Cultural Co-Operation of the Council of Europe, 1967), 236.

average pharmacology instruction: Marilyn Winterton Edmunds and Maren Steward Mayhew, *Pharmacology for the Primary Care Provider* (St. Louis: Elsevier, 2008), 19.

Chinese flight attendants: Jan Wong, *Jan Wong's China: Reports From a Not-So-Foreign Correspondent* (Toronto: Doubleday, 1999), 113.

Alcohol and Tobacco Tax division: *Cases Decided in the United States Court of Claims,* Vol. 177 (1976), 371.

teacher absences: Stephen L. Jacobson, "The Effects of Pay Incentives on Teacher Absenteeism," *The Journal of Human Resources* 24, no. 2 (1989): 283.

wage hours over the decade between 1979 and 1989: Lawrence Mishel et al., *The State of Working America: 1992–93* (Armonk: Sharpe, 1993), 131.

Belle E. Powers and Mrs. L.B. Carlisle: *Expenses and Disposition of Fees and Money Collected by State Officers and Departments for the Period from June 10, 1908 to June 30, 1919* (Des Moines: Emory English, 1910), 252–60.

John Self, Joe Shumake, and L.C. Watson: *Appendix to the House and Senate Journals of the Fifty-Second General Assembly, State of Missouri,* Vol. I (Jefferson, 1923).

120

Stewards on trains Numbers 5 and 6: *National Railroad Adjustment Board, Awards 1351 to 1450*, Vol. XII (Chicago: NRAB, 1941), 456–57.

Dunfermline and Glasgow passenger train: *Minutes of Evidence before the Royal Commission on Labour* (August 5, 1892), 346.

Simla to Madras: *Indian Statutory Commission Report* (New Delhi: Logos, 1930), 221.

East St. Louis Junction: *Proceedings* (Chicago: American Railway Association, 1927), 238.

detention of freight cars in Altoona: "Reconsignment Case," *The Traffic World* 21, no. 3 (January 19, 1918): 101.

the time cars in an eastern city were worked: *The Western Fruit Jobber*, Vol. XV (1928): 26–27.

harvests by hand in Campiña: James Simpson, "Technical Change, Labor Absorption and Living Standards in Rural Andalucía, 1886–1936," *Agricultural History* 66, no. 3 (Summer, 1992), 20.

the two-platoon system of firefighting: *Industrial Commission of New South Wales, The Industrial Abitration Reports*, Vol. XXXVII (Sydney: V.C.N. Blight, 1938), 56–58.

colleries around Nottingham: *The Labour Gazette*, August 1897, 243.

the lath industry in Wisconsin: "Manufacturers' Returns," *Labor and Industrial Statistics: State of Wisconsin, 1898–1899* (Madison: Democrat Printing Company, 1901), 531.

the monumental building projects of a toutorix: Raimund Karl, "**butācos, *uossos, *geistlos, *ambaχtos:* Celtic Socio-economic Organization in the European Iron Age," *Studia Celtica* 40, no. 1 (2006): 36.

erection of an institutional hospital: Herbert L. Flynn, "Why Have a Hospital within an Institution?" *Proceedings and Addresses of the Annual Session* 57 (American Association of Mental Deficiency, 1933), 303.

chronic-illness days: T.D. Crocker et al., "Experiments in the Economics of Air Pollution Epidemiology," in *Methods*

Development for Assessing Air Pollution Control Benefits, Vol. I (Washington, DC: Environmental Protection Agency, 1979), 148.

a frosted incandescent lamp: *Bulletin of the Bureau of Standards* 4, no. 1 (1907): 111–15.

operation surcharges for postponements: *Code of Federal Regulations, Title 33, Navigation and Navigable Waters, PT. 200-End, Revised as of July 1, 2013* (Washington: Federal Register, 2013), 748.

advance notice required by non-national fishing vessels: Food and Agriculture Organization of the United Nation, *Report of the FAO/GFCM Workshop on Port State Measures to Combat Illegal, Unreported and Unregulated Fishing* (Rome: U.N., 2007), 42.

corks in salt water: John Wilkinson, "A Course of Experiments to ascertain the Specific Buoyancy of Cork in different Waters: The respective Weights and Buoyancy of Salt Water and Fresh Water: And for determining the exact Weight of Human and other Bodies in Fluids," *Philosophical Transactions, Giving Some Accompt of the Present Undertakings, Studies, and Labours of the Ingenious in Many Considerable Parts of the World* (London: Royal Society, 1766), 100.

121

Hex river to the Swarte Berg: L.S. Faber et al., *The Record; or, A Series of Official Papers Relative to the Condition and Treatment of the Native Tribes of South Africa*, Part III, No. 1 (1770), 2.

express postal route from Berlin: Rolf Hosfeld, *Karl Marx: An Intellectual Biography* (New York: Berghahn Books, 2012), 57.

Marshall's School in Cambridge: "From the Clubs and Schools," *Flight International* 32 (1937): 316.

underwater endurance record: unsigned sidebar, *Contemporary Musicians* 65 (2009): 57.

Voice of America: *Voice of America: Management Actions Needed to Adjust to a Changing Environment* (US General Accounting Office, July, 1992), 53.

Radio Berlin International: Ian Greig, *The Communist Challenge to Africa: An Analysis of Contemporary Soviet, Chinese, and Cuban Policies* (Surrey: Foreign Affairs Publishing, 1977), 99.

ITV: unsigned memorandum, *Public Service Content* (London: Stationery Office, 2007), 111.

Trans-Canada network: Earnest Austin Weir, *The Struggle for National Broadcasting in Canada* (Toronto: McClelland and Stewart, 1965), 317.

survival time for the pigeon: Steven M. Horvath and G.B. Spurr, "Effects of Hypothermia on General Metabolism," in *The Physiology of Induced Hypothermia: Proceedings of a Symposium*, ed. Robert Dunning Dripps (Washington, DC: National Academy of Sciences, 1956), 8.

European Starlings: Ronald Eisler, *Handbook of Chemical Risk Assessment: Health Hazards to Humans, Plants and Animals, Vol. 2: Organics* (Boca Raton: Lewis, 2000), 862.

falconoid herpes virus: Jaime Samour, *Exotic Animal Medicine* (Edinburgh: Elsevier, 2012), 141.

medium-sized rice-field rats: A.P. Buckle, F.P. Rowe, and Y.C. Young, "Laboratory Evaluation of 0.025% Warfarin Against *Rattus argentiventer*," *Tropical Pest Management* 26 (1980): 163.

multipart hand-written forms: *Proceedings and Papers of the Annual Conference of the California Mosquito and Vector Control Association*, Vols. 50–54 (CMVCA Press, 1982), 47.

irradiated mice: P. Biscay et al., "Radiobiological Evaluation of a Newly Synthesized Cysteamine Derivative," *International Journal of Radiation Oncology, Biology, Physics* 12, no. 8 (August, 1986): 1470.

tame grouse: Peter Sharpe, Alan Woolfe, and Daniel Roby, "Raising and Monitoring Tame Ruffed Grouse (*Bonasa umbellus*) for Field Studies," *American Midland Naturalist* 139–40 (1998): 42.

West River (South Dakota) herd-harvest season: *South Dakota Game Report: Big Game Harvest Predictions* (2014), 51.

visiting zoos in Mississippi: E. Robert Daley, *State Comprehensive Outdoor Recreation Plan* (Jackson, 1990), 57.

olive leaf-moths: A.H. El-Kifl, A.L. Abdel-Salam, and A.M.M. Rahhal, "Biological Studies on the Olive Leaf-Moth, Palpita unionalis," *Bulletin de la Société entomologique d'Égypte* 58 (1974): 339.

Codling Moths: A.B. Fite, "Six Years of Life History Studies on the Coddling Moth," *New Mexico College of Agriculture and Mechanical Arts Bulletin* 127 (June 1921): 39.

female corn borers: W.C. O'Kane and P.R. Lowry, "The European Corn Borer: Life History in New Hampshire, 1923–1926," *New Hampshire Agricultural Experiment Station Technical Bulletin* 33 (1927): 17.

pre-pupal stage of bolls: David G. Rustico, "Biology of the Cotton Flowerweevil, Amorphoidea Lata Motschulsky (Coleoptera Curculionidae)," *Philippine Journal of Science* 122, no. 4 (1993): 332.

122

mean duration of shedding Herpes: D.S. Rootman et al., "Corneal Nerves Are Necessary for Adrenergic Reactivation of Ocular Herpes," *Investigative Ophthalmology & Visual Science* 29 (1988): 351.

rhesus monkeys with Yellow Fever: M.V. Hargett and H.W. Burruss, "The Use of Rhesus Monkeys in the Testing of Aqueous-Base Yellow Fever Vaccine," *Collected Papers on Yellow Fever,* Vol. VII (New York: Rockefeller Foundation, 1927), 168.

relapsing fever from bilious typhoid: Leo Popoff, "Relapsing Fever," in *Twentieth Century Practice: An International Encyclopedia of Modern Medical Science by Leading Authorities of Europe and America,* ed. Thomas L. Stedman, Vol. XVI (New York: William Wood and Company, 1899), 492.

charity patients with acute pediatric appendicitis: Harry Richter, "Surgery of the Gastro-Intenstinal Tract," in *Children Pediatrics,* Vol. III, ed. Isaac Abt (Philadelphia: W.B. Saunders, 1923), 579.

successive occupants of pernoctated ward beds: *Royal Hospital of St. Bartholomew, Report* (1872), 23.

cytomegalovirus infection in infants: R. Stefanov and B.D. Dimitrov, "Cytomegalovirus Infections in Infants: An Example of a Chronopharmacological Approach," *Folia Medica* 41, no. 1 (1999): 22.

period of menstrual flow in after life: *Transactions of the American Gynecological Society* (1876), 62.

administration of 6mg betamethasone: William Martindale, James E.F. Reynolds, and Ainley Wade, *Martindale: The Extra Phamacopoeia: Incorporating the Squire's "Companion,"* 26th edn. (London: The Pharmaceutical Press, 1972), 497; Bronwen Jean Bryant, Kathleen M. Knights, and Evelyn Salerno, *Pharmacology for Health Professionals* (Marrickville: Mosby, 1999), 558.

broncopulmonary complications: *Excerpta Medica: Pediatrics,* Section VII, Vol. XII (1958), 284.

L asparaginase: *Drug Facts and Comparisons* (1997), 3319.

zymotic and constitutional diseases: *Sanitary and Statistical Report of the Surgeon General of the Navy* (1882), 289.

exponentially increasing Synechococcus: *Canadian Bulletin of Fisheries and Aquatic Sciences* 214 (1979), 106.

cloudage between March and May: *Fourth Conference on Satellite Meteorology and Oceanography* (Boston: American Meteorological Association, 1989), 124.

last observation at Arica: Winslow Upton, "Geographical Position of the Arequipa Station," *Annals of Harvard College Observatory* 47, no. 9 (1903), 244.

Atlanta to Birmingham: *Interstate Commerce Commission Reports: Motor Carrier Cases. Decisions of the Interstate Commerce Commission of the United States,* Vol. 100 (1968), 554.

the time it takes volatile matter to decompose: William Joseph Oswald, *The Influence of Physical Environment Upon the Over-all Efficiency of Light-energy Conversion by Chlorella in the Process of Photosynthetic Oxygenation*, PhD Dissertation, University of California at Berkeley, 1957, 108.

the steeping time, in guano, of oats: "Great Annual Show of the Union Agricultural Society," *The Farmer's Magazine* 9 (1844): 492.

reaction time of buffered digesters: K. Niranjan, Marshall Rankowitz, and Martin R. Okos, *Environmentally Responsible Food Processing* (New York: America Institute of Chemical Engineers, 1994), 18.

oral ingestion of urea: *Excerpta Medica* (1959), 1257.

anerobic digestion of swine wastewater: P.Y. Yang and S.Y. Nagano, "Sludge Recycling," in *Transactions of the ASAE*, vols. 4–6 (St. Joseph: American Society of Agricultural Engineers, 1985), 1284, 1287.

123

Farfield from the Ridge: Luc Rainville, *Propagation of the Internal Tide from the Hawaiian Ridge*, PhD Dissertation, UC San Diego, 2004, 84.

the Sacramento and San Joaquin Rivers: Louis Theodore, "Simulation of Contaminants in Bays: Application to San Francisco Bay Complex," *Offshore Technology Conference* 3, no. 2 (1971): 565.

Croatia to Antwerp: unsigned tabulation, *Drewry Monthly* (1999): xxxv.

Toulouse to Béziers: unsigned notice, *New Monthly Magazine* 15, ed. Edward Bulwer Lytton (1825): 20.

new trades in equity index futures: Perry Kaufman, *Alpha Trading: Profitable Strategies That Remove Directional Risk* (Hoboken: John Wiley & Sons, 2011), 231.

number of Opposition days: *House of Commons Debates* 109–116 (2005), 4356.

German tourists in Rome: Paul Hofmann, *Rome: The Sweet Tempestuous Life* (London: Harvill, 1983), 236.

radiological and laboratory investigation reports: J.B. Saha, J. Mitra, and A. Mondal, "Length of Stay of In-patients of a Gynaecological Ward in a Sub-divisional Hospital in West Bengal," *Indian Journal of Public Health* 35, no. 3 (1991): 72.

half-life of Iodine 131: *California Bureau of Radiological Health, Radiological Health News*, Vol. 6 (1967), 5–6.

half-life of gallium: Edward Silberstein, *Bone Scintigraphy* (Mount Risco: Futura Publishing, 1984), 91.

the time it takes to read the Bible: Christin Ditchfield, *Route 66: A Trip Through the 66 Books of the Bible* (Greensboro: Carson-Dellosa, 2008), 163.

Chang cycle: Choon San Wong, *A Cycle of Chinese Festivities* (Singapore: Malaysia Publishing House, 1967), 12.

sound of its own making: Robert Morris, *Box with the Sound of Its Own Making* (1961), collection Seattle Museum of Art.

124

coronal suture of the skull itself: Rainer Maria Rilke, "Primal Sound," in *The Book of Music and Nature: An Anthology of Sounds, Words, Thoughts*, eds. David Rothenberg and Martha Ulvaeus (Middletown: Wesleyan University Press. 2001), 23.

125

signatures of Creation: Rainer Maria Rilke, *Letters of Rainer Maria Rilke*, Vol. II: 1912–1926, trans. Greene J. Bannard (New York: Norton, 1945), 391–92.

the point at which window glass will be shattered: United States Bureau of Standards, *The Effects of Sonic Boom and Similar Impulsive Noise on Structures* (Washington, DC, 1971), 8.

parachute payload system: John S. Preisser, Clinton V. Eckstrom, and Harold N. Murrow, *Flight Test of a 31.2-foot-diameter Modified Ringsail Parachute Deployed at a Mach Number of 1.39 and a Dynamic Pressure of 11.0 Pounds Per Square Foot* (Springfield: NASA, 1967), 8.

booster stage of the Saturn 1 rocket: Roger Bilstein, *Stages to Saturn: A Technological History of the Apollo/Saturn Launch Vehicles* (Washington, DC: NASA, 1980), 79.

landing gear of a lunar vehicle: Robert W. Herr and H. Wayne Leonard, *Dynamic Model Investigation of Touchdown Stability of Lunar-Landing Vehicles* (Springfield: NASA, 1967), 18.

nickel–copper alloy bars: Canadian Institute of Mining and Metallurgy, *Industrial Applications of Nickel* (1986), 132.

conservatively designed ram: J. Adolfsson and J. Karlsén, *Mechatronics '98* (Kidlington: Elsevier, 1998), 488.

mass of the earth: Guy Cavet Myhre, *Inertia Is Gravity* (Bloomington: AuthorHouse, 2004), 18.

the spine, when standing: Mario A. Gutierrez, *Understanding Low Back Pain: Breakthroughs and New Advances in the Diagnosis and Treatment of Low Back Pain* (Lincoln: iUniverse, 2005), 8–9.

force on bone plugs lacking helical threads: Mark R. McLaughlin, Regis Haid, and Richard Fessler, eds., *Lumbar Interbody Fusion Techniques: Cages, Dowels, and Grafts* (London: Taylor & Francis, 2008), 28.

intact monkey spinal columns: *Proceedings of the 26th Stapp Car Crash Conference* (San Francisco, 1981), 192.

force required to fracture the human skull: Noah Baird, *Donations to Clarity* (Kernersville: Cut Above Books, 2011), 1.

126

the column is a compass needle: Thomas Moynihan, *Spinal Catastrophism: A Secret History* (Falmouth: Urbanomic, 2019), 10 *et passim*.

psychogeophysical forces: London Psychogeophysics Summit, "What Is Psychogeophysics?" *Mute*, August 4, 2010, https://www.metamute.org/community/your-posts/what-psychogeophysics.

the birth of the science of geology: Jussi Parikka, *A Geology of Media* (Minneapolis: University of Minnesota Press, 2015), 69.

127

Body whose bones: "Corps dont les os ne sont plus et sont déjà rochers, le cœur plus et déjà vague, le ventre plus et déjà plage." Pierre Garnier, "Préface," in Ilse Garnier, *Blason du coprs féminin* (Paris: L'Herbe Qui Tremble, 2010).

128

snakes were born from the marrow of the spine: "sunt qui cum clauso putrefacta est spina sepulchro mutari credunt humanas angue medullas [Some believe that the human marrow of a putrefied spine, sealed in the tomb, turns into a snake]." Ovid, *Metamorphoses* XV, lines 389–90.

vascular stems: Mark Dion, "Robert Smithson Educational Filmstrip," in *Matthew Buckingham, Abraham Cruzvillegas, Mark Dion, Teresita Fernández, Trevor Paglen, Rayyane Tabet, Diana Thater on Robert Smithson,* eds. Atkins and Kivland, 68–69.

spiral columns unafraid of time: Darwin, *The Collected Writings of Erasmus Darwin,* 161.

caught in a physiological trap: qtd. in Eisley, *The Firmament of Time,* 159.

129

What then is the spinal column: Moynihan, *Spinal Catastrophism,* 31.

man-made systems mired in abandoned hopes: Smithson, "The Spiral Jetty," 146.

"formed stones": W.J. Sollas, "The Influence of Oxford on the History of Geology," *Science Progress: A Quarterly Review of Current Scientific Investigation,* eds. Sir Henry Burdett and J. Bretland Farmer, Vol. III (London: The Scientific Press, 1898), 31–32.

130

internal acoustic meatus: William W. Campbell, *DeJong's The Neurologic Examination* (Philadelphia: Lippincott Williams & Wilkins, 2005), 227.

lower frequencies: Daphne Manoussaki et al., "The Influence of Cochlear Shape on Low-frequency Hearing," *Proceedings of the National Academy of Sciences* 105, no. 16 (2008): 6162–66; Mark N. Colemand and Matthew W. Colbert, "Correlations between Auditory Structures and Hearing Sensitivity in Non-human Primates," *Journal of Morphology* 271, no. 5 (May 2010): 511–32.

131

the slap of their collision in the Pacific: Friedrich Kittler, "Lightning and Series — Event and Thunder," *Theory, Culture, and Society* 23, nos. 7–8 (2006): 69.

the need to avoid the facial nerve: M. Pietsch et al., "Spiral Form of the Human Cochlea Results from Spatial Constraints," *Scientific Reports* 7, no. 1 (2017): art. 7500.

132

bones of the human ear: Samuel Taylor Coleridge, *The Notebooks of Samuel Taylor Coleridge,* Vol. IV: 1819–1826, eds. Merton Christensen and Kathleen Coburn (London: Routledge, 1990), 255.

sonority of miniature mountain-ranges: Moynihan, *Spinal Catastrophism,* 235.

The conclusion I had hoped to reach: "Los hechos más disímiles pueden relacionarse de modo de participar en un mismo relato, y su incoherencia puede hacerse coherente. Si hay un llamado telefónico equivocado, va a llover, Si se para una paloma en la baranda del balcón, va a haber huelga en el subte. Si le cambian de nombre a un país, se va a morir un pariente. No hay restricciones, no hay temas vedados, el universo entero en sus innumerables manifestaciones está a nuestra disposición. La única restricción es el azar, que no restringe nada porque es lo que por definición lo permite todo y pone en comunicación los seres más alejados lo mismo que los más cercanos, atraviesa niveles, planos, lenguajes." César Aira, *Artforum* (Distrito Federal: Blatt & Ríos, 2014), 48.

133
the conduct of this Discourse: Poe, *Eureka,* 118–19.

Selected Bibliography

Aira, César. *Artforum*. Distrito Federal: Blatt & Ríos, 2014.

Arrivé, Michel. *Les langages de Jarry: essai sémiotique littéraire*. Paris: Klincksieck, 1973.

Atkins, Katherine, and Kelly Kivland. *Artists On Robert Smithson*. New York: Dia Art Foundation, 2020.

Bataille, Georges. *La part maudite*. Paris: Minuit, 1967.

Benjamin, Walter. *Gesammelte Schriften*. Edited by Rolf Tiedemann. Frankfurt-am-Main: Suhrkamp Verlag, 1977–1982.

Berardi, Franco "Bifo." *Breathing: Chaos and Poetry*. Intervention Series 26. South Pasadena: Semiotext(e), 2018.

Blake, William. *Complete Writings*. Edited by Geoffrey Keynes. London: Oxford University Press, 1966.

Breton, André. *L'amour fou*. Paris: Gallimard, 1937.

———. *Point du jour*. Paris: Imprimerie Crété, 1934.

Bridgman, Percy W. *The Nature of Thermodynamics*. Gloucester: P. Smith, 1969.

Bucur, Voichita. *Handbook of Materials for String Musical Instruments*. Switzerland: Springer, 2016.

Caillois, Roger. *L'écriture des pierres*. Paris: Flammarion, 1970.

———. *Pierres réfléchies*. Paris: Gallimard, 1975.

Carr, Annie Call. *East of Antelope Island*. Kaysville: Davis County Company, 1948.

Chakrabarty, Dipesh. "Postcolonial Studies and the Challenge of Climate Change." *New Literary History* 43, no. 1 (Winter 2012): 1–18. DOI: 10.1353/nlh.2012.0007.

Colemand, Mark N. , and Matthew W. Colbert. "Correlations Between Auditory Structures and Hearing Sensitivity in Non-Human Primates." *Journal of Morphology* 271, no. 5 (May 2010): 511–32. DOI: 10.1002/jmor.10814.

Darwin, Erasmus. *The Collected Writings of Erasmus Darwin.* London: Continuum, 2004.

Desnos, Robert. *Nouvelles Hébrides et autres textes, 1922–1930.* Paris: Gallimard, 1978.

Durham, Bill. "Sailors of the Briny Shallows." *Westways* 49 (Los Angeles: Automobile Club of Southern California, March, 1957).

Eiseley, Loren. *The Firmament of Time.* New York: Athaneum. 1966.

Fourier, Charles. *Publication des manuscrits de Fourier,* Vol. IV: 1857–1858. Paris: Librairie Phalanstérienne, 1858.

Fox, William L. *The Void, The Grid & The Sign: Traversing the Great Basin.* Reno: University of Nevada Press, 2016.

Garnier, Ilse. *Blason du coprs féminin.* Paris: L'Herbe Qui Tremble, 2010.

Giffin, Lawrence. *Untitled, 2004: a poem.* New York: After Hours Editions, 2020.

Heizer, Michael. *Sculpture in Reverse.* Los Angeles: MoCA, 1984.

Hirsch, Steven, and Lucien van der Walt. *Anarchism and Syndicalism in the Colonial and Postcolonial World, 1870–1940.* Leiden: Brill, 2010.

Hoffman, Bettina. *The Viola de Gamba.* Translated by Paul Ferguson. London: Routledge, 2018.

Isidorus Hispalensis. *Isidore of Seville's Etymologies: The Complete English Translation of Isidori Hispalensis Episcopi Etymologiarum sive Originum Libri XX.* Translated by Priscilla Throop. Charlotte: Medieval MS, 2005.

Israel, Nico. *Spirals: The Whirled Image in Twentieth-Century Literature and Art.* New York: Columbia University Press, 2015.

Jarry, Alfred."Commentaire pour servir à la construction pratique de la machine à explorer le temps." *Le Mercure de France* 110 (February 1899).

———. *Gestes et opinions du docteur Faustroll, pataphysicien.* Paris: Libraire Stock, 1923.

———. *L'amour absolu.* Paris: Mercure de France, 1952.

———. *Ubu Roi.* Paris: Mercure de France, 1896.

Jones, Katherine T. "Scale as Epistemology." *Political Geography* 17, no. 8 (1998): 25–28. DOI: 10.1016/S0962-6298(97)00049-8.

Kimball, Solomon F. "Early-Day Recollections of Antelope Island." *Improvement Era* 10, no. 5 (March 1907): 334–39.

Kittler, Friedrich. "Lightning and Series — Event and Thunder." *Theory, Culture, and Society* 23, nos. 7–8 (2006): 63–74. DOI: 10.1177/0263276406069883.

Klauber, Laurence Monroe. *Rattlesnakes: Their Habits, Life Histories, and Influence on Mankind.* San Diego: Zoological Society of San Diego, 1997.

Krauss, Rosalind, and Yves-Alain Bois. *Formless: A User's Guide.* New York: Zone Books, 1997.

Lafargue, Paul. *Le droit à la paresse.* Paris: Éditions Allia, 2005.

London Psychogeophysics Summit. "What Is Psychogeophysics?" *Mute*, August 4, 2010. https://www.metamute.org/community/your-posts/what-psychogeophysics.

Lowenhaupt Tsing, Anna. "On Nonscalability: The Living World Is Not Amenable to Precision-Nested Scales." *Common Knowledge* 18, no. 3 (Fall 2012): 505–24. DOI: 10.1215/0961754X-1630424.

Lucretius. *De Rerum Natura / On the Nature of Things.* Loeb Classical Library 181. Translated by W.H.D. Rouse. Cambridge: Harvard University Press, 1924.

Mallarmé, Stéphane. *Un coup de dés jamais n'abolira le hazard.* Paris: Gallimard, 1914.

Manning, Steven J. "The Fugitive-Pigment Anthropomorphs of Eastern Utah: A Shared Cultural Trait Indicating a Temporal Relationship." *Utah Rock Art* 23 (2003): 61–177.

Manoussaki, Daphne, Richard S. Chadwick, Darlene R. Ketten, Julie Arruda, Emilios K. Dimitriadis, and Jen T. O'Malley. "The Influence of Cochlear Shape on Low-frequency Hearing." *Proceedings of the National Academy of Sciences* 105, no. 16 (2008): 6162–66. DOI: 10.1073/pnas.0710037105.

McCaffery, Steve. *The Darkness of the Present: Poetics, Anachronism, and the Anomaly.* Tuscaloosa: University of Alabama Press, 2012.

Miller, David E. "Great Salt Lake: A Historical Sketch." *Utah Geological and Mineral Society Bulletin* 116 (June 1980): 3–24.

———. "Great Salt Lake and Its Islands." In *Great Salt Lake National Park in Utah.* Washington, DC: U.S. Government Printing Office, 1961.

MilNeil, Christian Neal. "Inner-City Glaciers." In *Making the Geologic Now: Responses to Material Conditions of Contemporary Life,* eds. Elizabeth Ellsworth and Jamie Kruse. Brooklyn: punctum books, 2013.

Minter, Adam. *Junkyard Planet: Travels in a Billion Dollar Trash Trade.* New York: Bloomsbury, 2013.

Molderings, Herbet. *Duchamp and the Aesthetics of Chance: Art As Experiment.* New York: Columbia University Press, 2010.

Morgan, Dale. *The Great Salt Lake.* Indianapolis: Bobbs-Merrill, 1947.

Moynihan, Thomas. *Spinal Catastrophism: A Secret History.* Falmouth: Urbanomic, 2019.

Nealon, Christopher. "Infinity for Marxists." *Mediations: Journal of the Marxist Literary Group* 28, no. 2 (Spring 2015): 47–64. https://www.mediationsjournal.org/articles/infinity-for-marxists.

Nierendorf, Karl. *Art Forms in Nature.* New York: Weyhe, 1935.

Palmer, Rosemary Gudmundson. *Jim Bridger: Trapper, Trader, and Guide.* Minneapolis: Compass Point Books, 2007.

Parikka, Jussi. *A Geology of Media.* Minneapolis: University of Minnesota Press, 2015.

Perloff, Marjorie. *The Futurist Moment: Avant-Garde, Avant Guerre, and the Language of Rupture.* Chicago: University of Chicago Press, 1987.

Pietsch, M., L. Aguirre Dávila, P. Erfurt, E. Avci, T. Lenarz, and A. Kral. "Spiral Form of the Human Cochlea Results from Spatial Constraints." *Scientific Reports* 7, no. 1 (2017): art. 7500. DOI: 10.1038/s41598-017-07795-4.

Poe, Edgar Allan. *Eureka: A Prose Poem.* Los Angeles: Green Integer, 2020.

Reynolds, Anne. *Robert Smithson: Learning from New Jersey and Elsewhere.* Cambridge: MIT, 2003.

Rilke, Rainer Maria. *Letters of Rainer Maria Rilker, Vol. II: 1912–1926.* Translated by G.J. Bannard. New York: Norton, 1945.

———. "Primal Sound." In *The Book of Music and Nature: An Anthology of Sounds, Words, Thoughts,* edited by David Rothenberg and Martha Ulvaeus. Middletown: Wesleyan University Press. 2001.

Rimbaud, Arthur. *Oeuvres Complètes.* Paris: Gallimard, 1954.

Ringholz, Raye Carleson. *Barrier of Salt: The Story of Great Salt Lake.* Salt Lake City: Deseret Book Company, 1970.

Roberts, Jennifer L. *Mirror-Travels: Robert Smithson and History.* New Haven: Yale University Press, 2004.

———. *Scale.* Chicago: University of Chicago Press, 2016.

Schreier, Christoph. "Nature As Art — Art As Nature." In *Karl Blossfeldt: Photography,* 11–21. Ostfildern: Cantz, 1994.

Segerman, Ephraim. "The Sizes of English Viols and Talbot's Measurements." *Galpin Society Journal* 48 (March 1995): 33–45. DOI: 10.2307/842801.

Shanken, Edward A. "Broken Circle &/ Spiral Hill? Smithson's Spirals, Pataphysics, Syzygy and Survival." *Technoetic Arts: A Journal of Speculative Research* 11, no. 1 (2013): 3–14.

Simpson, J.A., and E.S.C. Weiner. *The Oxford English Dictionary.* 2nd edition. Oxford: Clarendon Press, 1989.
Simpson, J.H. *Report of Explorations Across the Great Basin of the Territory of Utah.* Washington, DC: Government Printing Office, 1876.
Smith, Neil. "Geography, Difference and the Politics of Scale." In *Postmodernism and the Social Sciences,* edited by Joe Doherty, Elspeth Graham, and Mo Malek, 57–79 (New York: Palgrave, 1992).
Smithson, Robert. *Robert Smithson, The Collected Writings.* Edited by Jack Flam. Berkeley: University of California Press, 1996.
Stansbury, Howard. *An Expedition to the Valley of the Great Salt Lake of Utah: Including A Description of its Geography, Natural History, And Minerals, and an Analysis of Its Waters: With an Authentic Account of the Mormon Settlement.* Philadelphia: Lippincott, Grambo & Co., 1852.
Stum, Marlin. *Visions of Antelope Island and Great Salt Lake.* Logan: Utah State University Press, 1999.
Sullivan, Edward. T*he Book of Kells: Described by Sir Edward Sullivan, Bart., And Illustrated with Twenty-Four Plates in Colours.* 2nd edition. London: The Studio, 1920.
Sullivan, Robert. "The Source of Robert Smithson's Spiral." *The New Yorker,* June 18, 2014. https://www.newyorker.com/culture/culture-desk/the-source-of-robert-smithsons-spiral.
Thayer, William Makepeace. *Marvels of the New West: A Vivid Portrayal of the Stupendous Marvels in the Vast Wonderland West of the Missouri River.* Norwich: Henry Bill, 1887.
Topping, Gary. *Great Salt Lake: An Anthology.* Logan: Utah State University Press, 2002.
Van Alfen, Peter G. "Sail and Steam: Great Salt Lake's Boats and Boatbuilders, 1847–1901." *Utah Historical Quarterly* 63, no. 3 (Summer 1995): 194–221. https://www.jstor.org/stable/45062238.
Vilain, Robert. "Jugendstil." In *Encyclopedia of German Literature,* ed. Matthias Konzett, 543–46. Chicago: Fitzroy Dearborn, 2000.

Williams, Duncan. *The Other Side of Zen: A Social History of Sōtō Zen Buddhism in Tokugawa Japan*. Princeton: Princeton University Press, 2009.

Wittgenstein, Ludwig. *Remarks on the Foundations of Mathematics*, edited by G.H. von Wright, Rush Rhees, and translated by G.E.M. Anscombe. Cambridge: MIT Press, 1967.

Woolf, Virginia. *Monday or Tuesday*. New York: Harcourt, Brace and Company, 1921.

www.ingramcontent.com/pod-product-compliance
Lightning Source LLC
LaVergne TN
LVHW020043110826
845155LV00029B/622

* 9 7 8 1 9 5 3 0 3 5 6 4 6 *